Praise for
Convicted

"In *Convicted,* Mark Tabb has captured a story that illustrates the grace and redemption first modeled for the world by Christ on the cross. It's also a story of an improbable friendship that will challenge your assumptions and transform the way you see all those who might live on the other side of town. *Convicted* is a must-read for anyone who longs for the day when the dividing lines of race, class, and bigotry are finally overcome by the greater forces of love, forgiveness, and brotherhood."

—Rev. Samuel Rodriguez, president of the National Hispanic
Christian Leadership Conference and author of *Be Light*

"What an amazing story of the work the Holy Spirit can do in our lives when we allow him and the power of forgiveness to heal all wounds!"

—Daniel Muir, former NFL player with the Indianapolis Colts
and other teams

CONVICTED

A CROOKED COP, AN INNOCENT MAN, AND AN UNLIKELY JOURNEY OF FORGIVENESS AND FRIENDSHIP

JAMEEL MCGEE & ANDREW COLLINS

WITH MARK TABB

WATERBROOK

Convicted

This is a work of nonfiction. Nonetheless, some of the names of the individuals involved have been changed in order to disguise their identities. Any resulting resemblance to persons living or dead is entirely coincidental and unintentional.

Hardcover ISBN 978-0-7352-9072-3
eBook ISBN 978-0-7352-9073-0

Published in the United States by WaterBrook, an imprint of the Crown Publishing Group, a division of Penguin Random House LLC, New York.

WaterBrook® and its deer colophon are registered trademarks of Penguin Random House LLC.

Library of Congress Cataloging-in-Publication Data
Names: McGee, Jameel Zookie, author. | Collins, Andrew, 1982– author. | Tabb, Mark A., author.
Title: Convicted : a crooked cop, an innocent man, and an unlikely journey of forgiveness and friendship / Jameel Zookie Mcgee and Andrew Collins, with Mark Tabb.
Description: First edition. | Colorado Springs, CO : WaterBrook, 2017.
Identifiers: LCCN 2017016086| ISBN 9780735290723 (hardcover) | ISBN 9780735290730 (electronic)
Subjects: LCSH: Forgiveness—Religious aspects—Christianity. | Forgiveness of sin. | Interpersonal relations—Religious aspects—Christianity. | Friendship—Religious aspects—Christianity. | McGee, Jameel Zookie. | Collins, Andrew, 1982–
Classification: LCC BV4647.F55 M35 2017 | DDC 277.74/110820922—dc23 LC record available at https://lccn.loc.gov/2017016086

Printed in the United States of America
2017—First Edition

10 9 8 7 6 5 4 3 2 1

CONTENTS

AUTHOR'S NOTE

One hundred years ago, Benton Harbor was a growing town on Michigan's sunset coast. The city boasted a trolley system, college, and opera house, along with an amusement park and semipro baseball team, both sponsored by the religious commune the House of David. Benton Harbor was originally founded in 1860 as a lake port that specialized in exporting fruit. In the 1920s factories began sprouting and brought rapid growth. The landmark Hotel Vincent was built in 1926 with the eighth floor designed to accommodate its most infamous guest, Chicago gangster Al Capone. Mansions sprang up along Pipestone Avenue, which runs through the center of town. Benton Harbor continued to grow through the 1930s and 1940s as black families moved from the southern states to work in local factories.

By the 1960s the boom days were over. While Whirlpool kept its headquarters in Benton Harbor, most of the high-paying manufacturing jobs that had built the area simply disappeared. Racial tension grew. Most white residents moved to the other side of the St. Joseph River to the town bearing the same name. Some still refer to Benton Harbor and St. Joseph as twin cities, but they could not be more different. Today, Benton Harbor's population is over 90 percent black, while St. Joseph's is over 90 percent white. The median income in Benton Harbor is barely 30 percent that of St. Joseph and slightly more than one-third the national average. Nearly 40 percent of Benton Harbor households get by on less than $15,000 a year.

The streets and city services reflect the state of the city. Potholes cover most of the roads away from Main Street. Taxes are some of the highest in the state, even though most residents struggle to pay them.

The first racially charged riots hit Benton Harbor on August 30, 1966, following the shooting death of an eighteen-year-old black man, Cecil Hunt, by a white man. After three consecutive nights of rioting, Mayor Wilbert Smith asked Governor George Romney to send in the National Guard. Even with more than seventeen hundred troops converging on the city, full order was not restored until September 5.

The gulf between predominantly black Benton Harbor and white St. Joseph grew even wider over the next few decades. As more and more factories shut their doors and poverty gripped the city, drugs and gang violence spread. Even today, Benton Harbor has one of the highest murder rates per capita in the United States.

Racial tension and violence erupted again in 1991 when the body of a young black man, Eric McGinnis, was fished out of Lake Michigan. He had last been seen at a St. Joseph club where weeks before he had met and started dating a white girl. (Eric's case was chronicled in Alex Kotlowitz's 1998 book *The Other Side of the River.**) The night Eric disappeared, a white man claimed he saw Eric breaking into his car. The man chased him away and toward an off-duty white deputy sheriff. Even today, many in the town are convinced Eric was murdered.

Benton Harbor exploded once again in 2003 following the death of twenty-seven-year-old Terrance Shurn. A black man, Shurn died after crashing his motorcycle during a high-speed chase with white police officers who sought to cite him for not having current license plates. Two months earlier another black man, Arthur Partee, had died in a struggle when police attempted to arrest him for an outstanding traffic warrant.

The two cases brought to the surface nearly forty years of racial tension. After two nights of rioting, several homes and businesses were burned down. Rioters also targeted the fire trucks that attempted to extinguish the blazes. More than two hundred state police officers restored order, but the tensions never went away.

Nor did the presence of the state police. Members of the community believe the police unfairly target them. The riots also exposed the sense of hope-

---

* Alex Kotlowitz, *The Other Side of the River: A Story of Two Towns, a Death, and America's Dilemma* (New York: Anchor, 1998).

lessness and despair of a city racked by high unemployment, poverty, violence, and drugs. Politicians have long vowed to resolve the problems, but on the tenth anniversary of the 2003 riots, reporters found the problems that had sparked the riots still remained. Nothing of substance had changed for those who lived in Benton Harbor.

There are real attempts being made even today to improve the city. Not long after the 2003 riots, a Jack Nicklaus signature golf course, Harbor Shores, was built on the south end of the city near Lake Michigan. A resort hotel and spa soon followed, with an upscale housing edition planned as well. A December 15, 2011, *New York Times Magazine* story heralded the building of the golf course as a new day for Benton Harbor.* Civic leaders claimed the building of the course and hotel would bring in needed tourist dollars and increase the tax base of the city.

Perhaps that will someday be true. But to truly understand Benton Harbor, you need only drive to the corner of Broadway and Weld to Broadway Park. At first glance the park appears encouraging. A bright-green-roofed gazebo sits in the middle of the park with what appears to be fairly new playground equipment nearby. Basketball courts sit on one end of the park, with swing sets directly across. When you look closer, however, you notice the swing sets are missing swings and trash is scattered across the ground.

But that's not what sets Broadway Park apart.

Before you walk across the park from the corner of Broadway and Weld to the gazebo or slides or swing sets or basketball courts, you first pass a three-foot-tall water hydrant standing not far from the sidewalk. Officially known as a bury hydrant designed to keep from freezing up during the cold Michigan winters, the hydrant leans noticeably to one side. And in the middle of the hydrant, perhaps a foot below the handle, a steady stream of water shoots out of a hole in the side. Long ago someone tried to plug the hole with tape, but it didn't

---

* Jonathan Mahler, "Now That the Factories Are Closed, It's Tee Time in Benton Harbor, Mich.," *New York Times Magazine*, December 15, 2011, www.nytimes.com/2011/12/18/magazine/benton-harbor.html.

work. Now the tape pushes the water downward, where it collects at the bottom of the hydrant. In the summer the ground around the hydrant resembles a wetland. In the winter it becomes a skating rink. But no matter the time of year, the water continues to shoot out the side of the hydrant, just as it has for years.

Residents used to complain to city hall about the hydrant. After all, the homeowners around the park help pay the water bill, and they do not want to pay for water running out on the ground year-round. But the city has claimed it does not have the money to fix the leak or replace the hydrant, which would cost around fifty dollars at any home improvement store. Eventually people quit asking the city to do anything. Now the water runs and runs and runs, and people accept it because that's just the way things are in Benton Harbor.

To understand Benton Harbor and the hopelessness that seems to pervade the city, you need only visit the forgotten leaking hydrant in Broadway Park. The people in the community feel just as forgotten.

Convicted is only one story of life in Benton Harbor. Maybe its hopeful ending is just what this town—and all of us—needs.

—Mark Tabb
Spring 2017

PROLOGUE

Andrew

The crowd parted like the Red Sea. At first I could not see what was happening or why the hundreds gathered in Benton Harbor's Broadway Park for our church's Hoops, Hotdogs, and Hip-Hop Festival moved aside so quickly. But then I saw him. I recognized the face but I had trouble putting a name to it. Whoever he was, he was angry, angry enough that the crowd instinctively cleared a path for him. And he was heading straight toward me.

To be honest, I had expected someone like him, in an apparent rage, to come and find me. This was, after all, the first time I'd shown my face in the heart of Benton Harbor since my release from federal prison. A couple of people I'd arrested back when I was a policeman had already found me. I ran into one guy at a mall right before I went to prison. He thanked me for coming clean about what I'd done because it got him out of jail. The rest of these reunions had come after my release. I ran into people at the grocery store and at gas stations and anywhere I went in the area. Some tried to act tough when they first saw me, but they ended up just smiling and laughing because they'd gone free while I went to prison. A couple others had cussed me out for ruining their lives. One guy threatened to get even.

And now this.

I glanced around the park, looking for my five-year-old daughter. Bringing her to the park with me had seemed like a good idea when I left my house. *What can go wrong at a block party?* I thought. When my daughter asked if she could play on the swings with some other kids, I told her sure, have fun. Who wants to spend a day at the park watching her dad hand out snow cones? Now, as I watched this angry man march through the crowd, a little boy and another man struggling to keep up with him, I wished she were right next to me. Perhaps he might think twice about doing anything in front of a five-year-old girl.

The man walked straight up to me, stopped, and stuck out his hand. I took it. "Remember me?" he asked in a tone that sounded more like a threat than a question.

Somehow a name came to me. "Jameel McGee," I replied. His grip on my hand tightened when I said his name. I tugged back a little, which only made him grip down that much harder, to the point of pain. I half expected to hear my bones crunch.

I looked closely at Jameel to try to get a read on what he was about to do. While I was a cop I was pretty good at reading people. What I read in Jameel made me even more nervous. His jaw was clinched, the muscles pulsating on the side. I glanced over to the man who had come up behind him. He looked terrified, not of me, but of what was about to happen. Then there was the little boy, who seemed more interested in the snow cones than anything else. He was a little older than my daughter. *I hope she doesn't come over here right now,* I thought.

My mind raced. I had to do something to diffuse the growing tension, so I did what I had planned to do in exactly this situation: I apologized. "Jameel, man, I am so sorry for what I did to you. I, er, I was an addict back then, not to drugs, but to my own ego and making a name for myself. That caused me to do a lot of stuff I'm ashamed of now. I was a real messed-up person back then, and unfortunately, people like you paid the price for that. I am so sorry."

Jameel's expression did not change. His grip stayed tight on my hand. I couldn't feel my fingers.

"But I've got to tell you," I continued, "that I'm a new person today. That guy you're mad at, I'm mad at him too, because, you know, he threw away his career and he left his wife and daughter behind when he went to prison. But that guy's dead now. He was crucified with Christ. Today, I'm a new creation in Christ. I am a different man, one who is very, very sorry for what I did to you back then."

The whole time I was talking, I was staring at Jameel, looking for some sort of reaction, either good or bad. But there was nothing. His expression never changed and his grip never loosened.

When I finished my little speech, Jameel huffed a couple of times and sort of shook his head. He bit his lip and looked over toward the little boy, then back at me. Finally, without loosening his grip on my hand even a little bit, he nodded over toward the boy and said, "I need you to tell him why his daddy missed out on three years of his life."

I felt like I'd been kicked in the stomach. What was I supposed to say to *that*? I didn't have an answer. I couldn't give him back his time with his son that I had taken away from him. But I also thought perhaps we had made a little progress because he hadn't punched me in the face yet. I decided to build on that. I now knew the little guy was his son. Jameel is a dad and I am a dad, so I decided to connect with him on a dad-to-dad level. I wanted to let him know I understood his pain and frustration because I had felt it myself. So, like an idiot, I opened my mouth again.

"Jameel, man, I'm sorry. I know how you feel. I missed out on eighteen months of my daughter's life when I went to prison," I said.

Immediately, Jameel said, "I don't *care* what you missed out on."

I shut up. *You idiot!* I shouted at myself in my mind. *Why did you bring up your little eighteen-month slap on the wrist when he served three years because of you?*

I wanted to disappear, to grab my daughter, jump in my car, get out of Benton Harbor, and never come back. More than anything, I just wanted this to be over, not just my confrontation with Jameel, but all of it. I'd already quit one job when a customer recognized me as the guy who put him in prison and threatened to come back and shoot up the place. How many more times was I going to find myself face to face with someone who blamed me for ruining his life? And when might one of these meetings turn into something from which I could not walk away?

Jameel's jaw muscles kept flexing. The grip on my hand grew even tighter. He didn't just look angry. I saw a war going on inside this man, a war I believed was about to spill outside as well. The man with Jameel turned away like he didn't want to see what was about to go down. I braced myself. It had been a long time since someone had hit me in the face.

I hope my daughter doesn't see this, I thought.

1

FEBRUARY 8, 2006

Jameel

I knew I was taking a chance driving with a suspended license, which was why I was extra careful. I didn't speed. I didn't float any stop signs. I signaled before every turn. My taillights and brake lights all worked. The police should not have pulled me over, but this was Benton Harbor, and I am a black man, so I got pulled over anyway. The cop was cool, though. When he ran my license and found out it was suspended because of a couple of unpaid speeding tickets, he could have run me in. But he didn't. He handed me a ticket and told me to drive home and park my car until I paid my fines. *That's cool. Okay. I can do that.* I had no plans for the rest of the day anyway.

Even before the cop pulled me over I had planned on taking care of the tickets soon. A couple of months earlier I made a deal to open a car wash in Michigan City, Indiana, as soon as the weather warmed up in March. Before making the deal, I did a test run. I did more than wash cars. My shop did full-car detailing, both inside and out. I worked twelve hours or more a day, but that was all right with me. Owning my own business and being my own boss had been my dream all my life.

Most of the paperwork was signed, and I had only a few details left to take care of before I opened up the shop for good the next month. The last thing I was going to do was let some unpaid speeding tickets keep me from driving forty minutes each day between Benton Harbor and Michigan City to run my business. I definitely planned to take care of them in time to open my car wash.

After the cop let me leave, I drove over to my grandma's house where I was staying and decided to just chill for the rest of the day. Some of my cousins were there, along with some of their friends, most of whom I didn't know. There is always a crowd at my grandma's house. I've got a ton of cousins, and some of them were always around. That wasn't a big deal for me.

I hooked up my PlayStation 2 and started playing some games. One of my cousins came in and played a couple of games with me. He told me he really liked my game system. "Why don't you sell it to me?" he asked.

I told him, "No man, I don't think so."

"I'll give you a hundred bucks right now," he said.

"All right, sold." I needed the cash to pay off my tickets. Between that and the money I had from a check I'd just cashed from another job, I had about all I needed to pay them off.

After I sold the game to my cousin, we kept on playing. This was pretty much all I had planned for the day until one of my brothers, Buck, called to tell me he'd just talked to my ex.

I'd had a long-term girlfriend, but we had broken up over a year before.

"Yeah, what did she say?" I asked.

"She wants to bring your baby boy over to see you today, this afternoon," Buck said.

"Wow, man, finally," I said, excited. My ex and I had dated and then lived together for quite a while. However, things between us started falling apart when we found out she was pregnant. I started working extra-long hours so I could take care of my new family. At the time I worked a couple of different jobs. This was before the opportunity for the car wash came up. She didn't like my working so much and eventually everything just fell apart. She took off and

I had not seen her since. I didn't even know she'd had the baby until long afterward. This was going to be my first time to see my son.

"Yeah, I know it," Buck said. "So she's going to bring him over to see you, and I don't know, she might leave him with you for the day or maybe a couple of days."

"Okay," I said. "I'll be ready."

When I hung up the phone, I went to my room and changed my clothes and got ready to meet my son for the first time. I was nervous and excited at the same time. I checked out the kitchen and we didn't have a lot in there. Since I did not know how long I might have my son, I figured I needed to run to the store to pick up a few things. Going to the store presented a real problem. If I drove to the little neighborhood convenience store that was only a half mile from my grandma's house and got pulled over, I'd probably be arrested for driving with a suspended license. If that happened, there was no way I'd see my son. If my ex showed up and I wasn't here, she'd leave and not wait for me. But if my ex brought my son over and the cupboard was bare, I might not see him again for a long time either because she would think I was not able to take care of him.

I had to go to the store, but I could not drive. Not a problem, I thought. I had some cousins and their friends there in the house and they had cars. "Any of y'all want to give me a ride to the store real fast?" I asked.

One of the guys in the house, a guy named Will who knew one of my cousins, said, "Yeah. I'm fixing to go. I'll take you."

"All right, cool," I said. I got up to leave right away, which is what I needed to do, but he kept messing around, doing something, I don't know what. To be honest, I could have walked to the store and back by the time he was finally ready to go. I didn't say anything because I was the one asking for a ride.

Finally, he said, "You ready? Let's go." We drove to the store in his silver Dodge Durango. He drove. I rode in the passenger seat. Will had come over from Detroit, and the back of the car was full of his stuff.

When we pulled up to the store, Will asked me, "Can I borrow your phone?" Actually he asked before we even got to the store.

"Sure, man," I said. I figured that was the least I could do since he had given me a ride. He parked the car. I handed Will my phone and went into the store. This was not going to be a long shopping trip. I wanted to get in and out and back to my grandma's house as quickly as possible. For all I knew my ex was already there with my little boy. *Little boy!* The thought of that caused a smile to break free on my face. I picked up some milk, chips, pop, and gummy worms and went to pay for them. Gummy worms were my thing back then. *Will had better be ready to go as soon as I get out of here,* I thought. I didn't have a minute to spare.

The outside of the store looked completely different when I walked out with my stuff. The parking spots that had been empty a few minutes earlier were now full of cars. People were walking around. I paused for a moment. A guy walked up to the door, but he didn't act like he wanted to go into the store. He was coming after me. I know this because I stepped aside a little and he got right in my face. *Wow, what's going on?* I thought.

"Where's the dope, man?" the guy said.

"You can't be talking to me," I said.

"Yeah, I'm talking to you. Where's the dope?"

I didn't say anything. I didn't have time for this mess. I just started walking back to where Will had parked his Durango at the side of the store.

The guy blocked my way. "You got something for me?" he said.

I just shook my head, annoyed.

Then he reached into his shirt and pulled out a badge that was hanging on a chain around his neck. "You got something for me?" he asked again.

"I don't know what you're talking about," I said and kept on walking. That's when I saw Will standing outside the Durango on the passenger side of the car. *Why is he on that side?* I wondered.

Before I could ask Will anything, the guy I now knew was a cop pulled me over to the police car in front of the store. "Hands on the hood," he said.

"You serious?" I asked.

"Yeah. Hands on the hood."

I did as I was told, but all I could think was how I didn't have time for this. Not now. If my ex showed up at my grandma's house and I wasn't there, I might never get to see my son. I set my bag of groceries down and leaned against the car hood. The cop patted me down. He reached into my front jeans pocket and pulled out the cash I had from selling my PlayStation and cashing my check. I think I had somewhere around $500 on me. I never saw that money again.

"He's clean," the cop said to another officer standing nearby.

"Yeah I'm clean. I told you I was clean. Can I get out of here now? I gotta get home," I said. That wasn't all I said, but this is a family book. I was starting to get mad. When you're a black man in Benton Harbor, getting hassled by the police is just a part of life. I can't tell you how many times I've been pulled over for driving while black or how many times the cops searched me while I was walking down the street, minding my own business. It happens all the time. But this day I didn't have time for this nonsense. I had to get home.

"Get in the back of the car," the cop insisted.

"What!? You don't have any reason to arrest me," I said. "I *need* to get home."

"Get in the car," he said again. He didn't cuff me or anything like that, which was a good thing. If he had cuffed me I might have lost it. The whole thing was garbage. He had no reason to stop me or search me or hold me in this car. But I got in the back of the car like I was told. I knew what happens to those who don't.

After putting me in the car, the cop went over to Will's Durango. He said something to Will, then turned him around and cuffed him. The cop then brought Will over to the car and put him in the back seat next to me. As soon as the cop was out of earshot I asked Will, "What is going on, man?"

"Shh, shh . . . they got cameras on," Will said.

"I ain't got nothin' to do with none of this stuff. What is the problem? Why am I sitting in the back of this police car with you, man?"

"Just . . . Just wait. I gotta . . . you know . . . We can get over to the county lockup and we can . . . uh . . . bond out."

"Bond out?" I said. "I'm not going to county for anything. We need to clear this up now so I can get home."

"Yeah, man, we can bond out and then I'm going to run," Will said like he hadn't heard a word I'd said.

I felt like I was about to explode. "What are you even talking about? What is going on? What did you do?"

"Shh, man. Don't say nothing. They got cameras on us."

Several cops gathered around the Durango. I knew they were searching it, but that didn't matter to me. It wasn't my car. The back of the car was full of Will's stuff. I'd never been in it before he gave me the ride to the store. The only possible thing they could find in it was my cell phone, which I needed right now in case my brother called me with news about my ex and my baby son.

A couple of minutes later the cop who put me in the back of the car came walking back over to his police car. He had a stupid smile on his face. In his hand he held a baggie with what looked like some rock inside, that is, crack cocaine. He waved it at me and said, "Gotcha."

I shrugged and gave him an "I don't care" look. So he'd found crack cocaine in Will's car. That had nothing to do with me. I didn't know Will. I didn't know what he was into. He was going to get arrested and might do some real time for something like this, but it had nothing to do with me.

The cop came closer. "What's your name?"

I said nothing.

"Where do you live?"

I didn't reply.

"You got a Social Security number?"

Silence.

"All right. You don't want to talk. That's fine with me, but eventually you'll have to. You're under arrest for possession of crack cocaine with intent to distribute."

I could not believe my ears. I looked at Will, who didn't say a word. He knew this wasn't my dope and he could have cleared the whole thing up right then and there, but he didn't say a word. I looked back over at the cop.

"This is BS," I said. "I ain't got nothing to do with that dope you found. That's not my dope. That's not even my car."

"Yeah, right," the cop said.

I did not see my baby son that day. I didn't get to see him until he was five years old. I also didn't know who this cop was—not yet. I soon found out his name: Andrew Collins. For the next three years, not a day went by that I didn't think about my son who I had never seen and the cop who had kept me from him. And for most of those three years, I promised myself that if I ever saw this cop again, I was going to kill him. I intended to keep that promise.

2

A GOOD COP

Andrew

I woke up on the morning of February 8, 2006, determined to go out and make a big drug bust. As a relatively new narcotics officer, I had the same goal every day. I'd been on the Benton Harbor Police Department for a little over two years, and already I'd made a name for myself as one of the most aggressive narcotics officers on the force. Even when I worked on patrol, I made a lot of drug busts. That's what got me moved up the food chain. I bragged that I could tell if someone had drugs on them just by looking at them.

Claiming I could spot a drug dealer on sight wasn't nearly as big a deal as it sounds since I worked in Benton Harbor. Our department patrolled an area of only four square miles, but within that small area we had more drug houses and drug use than probably anywhere in America. On some of the streets I patrolled, you couldn't throw a rock without hitting a drug house or someone with dr[ugs in] their pockets. Early on I learned the jump-ou[t...] flushing drug users or dealers. Anytime I saw [...] individuals congregating in one area, I stopped m[...]

car, jumped out, and quickly walked over to the group. If anyone ran, I assumed they had drugs on them. In my first year on the force, I was involved in over one hundred foot chases and lost only five.

The only problem with the jump out was that when someone ran, they dropped whatever drugs they might have had on them. By the time I caught up with them, they were clean. I still arrested them for resisting an officer, but I was frustrated I couldn't pin anything bigger on them when I knew for a fact they were guilty. After all, if they weren't guilty, why did they run? I learned to retrace my steps and find whatever drugs the fleeing suspect had thrown down. Unfortunately, finding a bag of crack in the bushes does not constitute proof that the guy I was chasing had thrown it. And if I couldn't connect them directly to the drugs on the ground, the drug charges disappeared and I was back to having nothing more on them than resisting an officer.

I learned my way around this minor technicality when a prosecutor asked me, "Are you *sure* you didn't see him throw the drugs down while you were chasing him?" The way the prosecutor framed the question told me the answer he wanted to hear. "Oh yeah," I'd say, "I did see him throw something in that bush and I can confidently say that something was a bag of crack." Yes, that was lying under oath, but I really felt I had no choice because of the system. When I knew a suspect was guilty, I wasn't about to let him get off on a technicality. No good cop would; at least that's how I justified my actions to myself.

I never really thought about how my actions might impact the relationship between the police department and the people of Benton Harbor. Long before I arrived, those relations were already strained. In fact, the day I was supposed to join the department in June 2003 was pushed back after a high-speed police chase in town ended tragically. White police officers tried to pull over a black ian on a motorcycle because his license plate was expired. The man took off ¹ the officers chased him. The chase reached speeds of more than one hun- miles per hour before the motorcyclist crashed into a house and died. Harbor erupted into violence, not so much because of the man's death, se it was the latest in a long line of such actions by the overwhelm- police department in a town that is 95 percent black.

And that wasn't the first time the city had broken down into violence over tension with the police. The first race riots took place back in the 1960s when George Romney was the governor. He sent in the National Guard to restore order.

Honestly, nothing had really changed from the sixties until the time I joined the department. I had even been warned when I was a student at the police academy not to take a job in Benton Harbor. I tried to find a job elsewhere. I sent out eighty résumés when I graduated. Only two places replied. Benton Harbor was the first to offer me a job, so I took it. I was willing to go anywhere to fulfill my lifelong dream of becoming a police officer.

When I was five or six, my dad, who was really my stepdad, started hitting my mom. The police arrived and made everything right. The officer who came that night took my mom and me and my little brother to a safe place. He let me ride in the front seat of the patrol car and even use his siren.

After that I never wanted to be anything except a cop. Now that I was one, I was good at it. I made a lot of arrests and I put a lot of bad people behind bars. Every day when I woke up I was determined to put a few more away. That was especially true on February 8, 2006.

When I started my patrol that morning, I headed off to one of the streets where I knew drug activity occurred. On the outside it didn't look like a drug hot spot. Benton Harbor looks like a lot of small towns in the Midwest, with houses built around the turn of the century. Tall, mature trees line every block. Looks are deceiving. The drug trade took over the city long before I got there. The town is poor, city services are meager, and the unemployment rate was at least 25 percent when I moved there. Just across the St. Joseph River, it is a different story completely. The town of St. Joseph butts up against Benton Harbor. It is a resort town on the banks of Lake Michigan. Tourists flock to its Main Street with quaint shops and restaurants. Back then tourists rarely drove across the bridge to Benton Harbor. St. Joseph is also over 90 percent white with a median family income three times that of Benton Harbor.

I hadn't been on patrol long when I spotted what I was looking for. Up

ahead was a solitary man on a street known to be a drug hot spot. I stopped my
car, got out, and headed toward him. He didn't run. Maybe it was too cold for
that kind of thing or maybe he just recognized me because the two of us had
had several encounters in the past. I searched him and found a quarter ounce
of crack in one of his pockets. A quarter ounce is about equal to a handful of
M&M's, not by weight but in size.

"What are you doing with these drugs?" I asked.

"Well, uh, you know," he said.

"Get in the car," I said. I didn't want to spend any more time out in the
open talking to my suspect than I had to in case someone happened to see us.
Confidential informants don't stay confidential when people in town see them
talking to cops.

My suspect climbed into the back of the car.

"So what's it going to be?" I said. "You want to go to jail or go home?"

"Home," he said, which was music to my ears. "I don't want to go to jail."
That meant he was willing to cooperate.

"So what can you get me?" I asked.

"I can order you an ounce from Ox," he said. Ox was the street name for a
dealer. Everyone in Benton Harbor has a street name. I didn't know who Ox
was, but an ounce of crack is a big bust. It had a street value of nearly $2,800.
If I could nail someone dealing that size of rock, this would be one of my biggest busts ever. In terms of jail time, the feds consider an ounce of crack to be
the equivalent of one hundred times the same amount of powder cocaine. That
is, an ounce of crack equals nearly three kilos or close to six pounds of powder.
This had the potential to be a major, major bust.

"All right. We're going to go over to the police station and you can make
the call. If the buy goes through, you go home. If not, you know how this plays
out," I said.

"I'll get you Ox," he said.

I drove my suspect to the police station and listened in as he called Ox to
set up the drug deal. My new informer put the phone on speaker: "I'll bring

you a zone and meet you at the spot," I heard Ox say. "It's going to take me a little bit to put it together, but I'll call you back when I'm ready."

A zone is street talk for an ounce. I wasn't sure what the spot was, but the fact he didn't give an exact location told me these two had done business before. This was shaping up to be a great day.

Quite a bit of time went by without Ox calling my informant back. Finally, I told my guy, "Look, man. It looks like this isn't going to happen. You're going to jail."

"No, no, no, Collins, I'll call him back. This is going to happen." That's when his phone rang. "I'm here now," the voice on the other end said.

"Okay, okay, okay," my guy said. "I'll be right there." When he hung up the phone, my informant said, "He's going to be in a silver Durango at the convenience store on North Fair Street."

When I pulled up to the store, I saw the silver Durango just where my informant said it was supposed to be. A black man sat in the passenger seat. I walked over to him, which made him appear to become nervous. Even though he was still in the vehicle, I could tell he was a smaller man. I did not know Ox, but I had been told he was a big guy. This guy didn't fit the description. But since he was right where my informant told me he was going to be, I went ahead and confronted him. "I need you to get out of the car," I said.

The man looked me over and didn't move.

As a narcotics officer I was in plain clothes, not a uniform. "Police officer," I identified myself. "I need you to get out of the vehicle." He complied this time. The man was small and had some trouble getting out of the car because of some sort of disability that appeared to me to be cerebral palsy or something like it. Once I had him out of the car, I said, "I've got some information saying that you brought drugs here to sell."

"I don't know what you're talking about," the man said.

"Are you Ox?" I asked.

"No man. I ain't Ox. Ox is in the store."

Right then the door of the store opened and out walked a man I was certain was Ox. Two other police cars had arrived by this time. I nodded toward one of the other officers as I walked up to Ox as if to say, *That's our man*.

"Where's the dope, man?" I asked Ox. He acted like he didn't know what I was talking about, so I asked him again. "Where's the dope?" Ox tried to walk away from me, so I blocked his way. "You got something for me?" I said. When he acted like he didn't hear me, I pulled out my badge and asked him again. "I said, you got something for me?"

"I don't know what you're talking about."

I didn't have time to play this game. I could not let Ox get past me, or the dope he had to have on him might disappear. "Hands on the hood," I said. I searched him. He had some money in his front pocket, which fit the pattern of drug dealers. They always carried rolls of cash. However, I did not find any crack. Another officer came over to me. "He's clean," I said, more out of frustration than anything else. I knew this guy was carrying. I'd heard him make the arrangements to sell an ounce to my informant. That dope had to be here somewhere.

"I told you I was clean," Ox said. I didn't need to hear that. I had never arrested anyone who admitted they were guilty. Everyone was always clean.

"Get in the car," I said. Ox argued, so I repeated "Get in the car" in a way that made it clear this was not a request.

I walked back over to the guy next to the Durango. "What's your name?"

"Reginald," he said.

"Turn around, Reginald," I said.

I cuffed him and then put him in the back of my squad car next to Ox. I then called the prosecutor's office to make sure I wouldn't mess this bust up. I wanted to search the car, but I didn't know if I had probable cause. I didn't have a warrant and there wasn't time to get one. I needed to find a legal way to search the vehicle so that anything I found in it could be used in court against these guys. I explained the situation to one of the prosecutors. "I'm not sure what to do," I said.

"Hmm," he said. "Wait a minute. Do you smell marijuana? Maybe see what appears to be a seed?"

"Yeah, I think I smell marijuana," I replied.

"There's your probable cause," he said.

I smiled. "That's all I need," I said. I opened the door of the Durango and leaned in. Right away I spotted what I was looking for in the cup holder. I reached in and pulled out a baggie with a large rock of crack about the size of a softball. "Just what I ordered," I said.

I picked up the baggie and walked back to my car. Ox was looking at me, so I waved the baggie in his direction and said, "Gotcha." He turned away, clearly angry, which only made me that much happier. He knew I had him. I think he shrugged his shoulders at me, which convinced me even more that he was guilty. This was Ox and this was his dope and this was now a huge bust for me. An ounce of crack would bring in the feds, which would be even better for me. The feds didn't take on any cases they couldn't win, and if I gift wrapped one for them, well, that was a real boost to my career and my reputation. Needless to say, I was riding high.

I transported Ox to the police station. He refused to speak throughout the ride or at the station. That didn't matter. I found his name easily enough, Anthony R. I needed the name to write my arrest report.

Ox refused to talk, but Reginald was eager to spill his guts. I started to read him his rights, but he told me he knew them and he was ready to talk. "That dope wasn't mine," he said. "I picked the other dude up at a house over on Columbus Street. He told me he needed to drop off some crack to a dude at a store. I figured since it wasn't my dope, it didn't involve me, so I went ahead and gave him a ride."

"So it was definitely his dope?" I asked.

"Yeah," he said. "I heard him call his guy on the way over to the store. That was his rock in the cup holder."

That was all I needed. However, when I went back to my office to write the report, I knew I had a problem. Reginald could say it was Ox's crack, but since I never saw the drugs in Ox's possession, this was just Reginald's word against his. I never actually saw Ox in the car or near the drugs. While I had no doubt that the drugs belonged to Ox and that he was the one who had set up the buy, this discrepancy might keep me from getting a conviction, and I wasn't going to let that happen. Therefore, I made a few modifications to the narrative in my report to keep any unnecessary questions from coming up.

Nothing major. Just a couple of things. First, I wrote that I observed the defendant, Ox, in the passenger seat of the Durango when I arrived, with Reginald in the driver's seat. I then wrote that I approached the vehicle and ordered both men to put their hands up. "I observed the defendant move toward the center console, then straighten up and raise his hands," I added.

Modifying the report to fit the needs of the prosecutor didn't cause me any moral conflict. I knew Ox was guilty. When I checked his cell phone, which Reginald had in his possession when I pulled up, I found a call to my informant. That settled any questions of guilt in my mind. The worst thing I could possibly do, I believed, was to allow someone I had caught red handed to get off because of reasonable doubt. When you catch someone with drugs, there is no doubt. With my report I simply removed any that might have remained.

I woke up that morning hoping to make a big bust. Not only had I reached my goal for the day, but I also had nailed a very big fish who was now staring at some serious, maybe even federal, prison time.

All in all, a pretty good day.

3

MISTAKEN IDENTITY

Jameel

I could not believe I had been arrested again. The whole thing felt unreal, like a really bad dream. I had not done anything wrong except be in the wrong place at the wrong time with the wrong guy. Now I was the one in jail. When I got in the car with Will, I thought he might be up to something, but that didn't mean anything to me. That was his business. He did his thing and I did mine. All I needed was a ride.

This wasn't the first time I'd been arrested for something I didn't do. When I was fifteen I was living with my dad. A couple of my friends came by our house kind of late and asked if I wanted to go for a ride. I looked outside and they had a pretty nice car. "Cool. I'm in. Let's go," I told them.

My dad, however, had other ideas. He stopped me at the door and asked, "Where are you going?"

"I'm about to go hang out with Drew. He got his dad-dy's car and I'm fixing to go hang out."

"I don't think you should go. You should just stay home and chill. You've got a big week coming up. You're about to graduate. Leave the hanging out to them," he said.

Even though I was only fifteen, I was about to graduate from high school. I was a very good student. I hoped to go on to college and do something related to music. My dad knew my big plans, which is why he was trying to stop me. I also had no business going out because I'd broken my foot playing ball and had to hobble around on crutches.

Of course, I didn't listen. "Nah, Dad, I'll be all right. I'm cool."

"I'm telling you, Son, stay here. Them boys are gonna get you in some trouble. Whose car is that anyway?"

"That's his dad's car."

"You sure?" my dad asked.

"Yeah, Dad, I'm sure," I said. "Don't worry. I ain't gonna do nothing. You know I don't drink and I don't smoke and I don't do drugs. I ain't going to do anything to get myself in trouble. I'm just riding with them. Nothing more."

Reluctantly, my dad let me leave. I hobbled out of the house and got in the car with my buddies. We'd gone about a block when a police car pulled up behind us with its lights and siren on. As it turns out, my friends had stolen the car from some guy at knifepoint. I tried to tell the police officers that I had nothing to do with the carjacking, that I got in the car afterward, but it didn't matter. The victim even said I was innocent, but no one listened.

The prosecutor told my mother I was being charged as an adult with attempted murder and carjacking and two or three other crimes that were going to land me in jail for decades. Without asking me, she pleaded guilty for me to the lesser charge of receiving stolen property. At my sentencing I begged the judge and told him that I was a really good student and that I was about to graduate from high school. He told me I was going to graduate in prison, and just like that, *boom,* I received a three-year sentence and was sent off to an adult prison.

I grew up that day. I had to. My childhood was over.

It was a short childhood.

When I was little, both my parents used cocaine. That's why I hate drugs. There were times we did without food and shoes and other essentials because all the family money went to buying drugs.

My mom got off drugs before my dad. She found Jesus and started going to a church that stressed verses like "Spare the rod, spoil the child." After that my mother did not spare the rod. My twin brother, Jamal, and I were the two youngest, and we took the brunt of the beatings. Both of us ran away to escape from her. Usually we went straight to our grandma's house. That was my safe place. If my grandma was out of town, we stayed on the streets. A few times we were placed in foster homes, which was a really bad experience.

My dad finally got clean, but he ended up in jail before that happened. Once he got out, he fought to get custody of us. Eventually that happened, which was when I finally got to experience a real childhood. But then I woke up one day and was in prison with men a lot older than me for something I did not do.

My rough childhood had prepared me for prison life. When I was a kid, Jamal and I learned to box. Even though I'm not a big guy, I can take care of myself. You have to know how to fight in prison, but I also had to defend myself on the streets of Benton Harbor. The town was rough, real rough. When I was a young teenager, gangs got real heavy in town. You had to be careful not to wear the wrong colors or go into the wrong part of town with the wrong people. Fights were the least of the problems I faced. I had friends who got shot and killed. One good friend was just walking down the street one day when a car pulled up next to him and the people in the car opened fire with an AK-47. He had so many holes in him that he looked like swiss cheese. That told me I better be constantly aware of everything going on around me. If I wasn't, I might end up dead like my friend.

That's how I was in prison too. I walked in the gates and immediately went into survival mode. I was aware of everything around me, and I carried myself like a man, not a scared boy. There was also a lot of anger boiling inside me, but I could not let that get ahold of me or I might do something stupid and end up hurt or dead.

I was lucky because some of the older guys liked me and wanted to make sure I got out of prison the way I came in and that I never came back. They taught me the culture in the prison and helped me process the experience and just stay out of people's way. I got my GED while I was in there. Before I was arrested, I wanted to go to college, but that dream pretty much died the day the judge sentenced me to three years.

The biggest change that resulted from that first trip to prison was my relationship with God. Before I was arrested, I didn't want to have anything to do with church because my mom was really into a church that taught a lot of rules, rules that got me a beating if I didn't follow. She was so into her church that she went every single day and made us go with her. If we didn't, we got a beating. Every day but Sunday my siblings and I were the only kids there, but that didn't bother my mother. She was going to make sure we stayed on the right path, and if we strayed, we got a beating.

It didn't take me long to decide that if that's what God and church were about, I didn't want anything to do with them. But when I went to chapel services in prison, everything was different. In prison, nobody tries to prove anything or come across like they are the greatest, holiest Christians ever. A lot of people in the churches I went to as a kid seemed to worry more about what everyone else thought of them than what God thought. Prison church life was just the opposite. It's just you and God.

God used my time in prison to get my attention. I went to church services nearly every week, and I liked what I heard. Everything was just real. Right before I got out I took the next step and prayed to give my life to Jesus Christ. I was eighteen. I pretty much meant what I prayed, but I think I made the decision more for the other people in my life than for myself. I wanted to show them that I had changed, and this was the way to do it.

My parole was approved after I had served a little over two years. When I got out of prison, I left God there. It wasn't something I immediately did. It just sort of happened over time.

When I got back home, I went back to my old friends and started looking for a job. I did not go to church. Like I said, I didn't think highly of churches outside of prison. Most people there came across as fake to me. I didn't need that. So I got a job and got on with my life.

I made some changes in my life as well. For starters, I never got into a car with anyone I didn't know really, really well. No one. I made an exception to that rule on February 8, 2006, which was how I ended up in trouble again.

I had gone back to prison for a short time in between my getting out the first time and being arrested by Andrew. My brother and I had gone over to a cousin's house. We hadn't been there but a few minutes when the police raided the place. My cousin had drugs in the house and they carted him off to jail. I got sent back to prison for a parole violation, even though I had nothing to do with his drugs and had no idea they were even there. Again, I was at the wrong place at the wrong time. That happens a lot in places like Benton Harbor to a lot of people. You are guilty by association. It doesn't matter what you did or didn't do. If you are there, you're guilty. Case closed.

I reconnected with God when I went back to prison for my parole violation. I started reading my Bible and found some friends there who helped me work through the questions I had about who God is and what it means to live for him. I still had a lot of anger inside me because here I was, back in prison, for violating my parole over a conviction of a crime I did not do. I had tried to do things the right way, but because I got in a car I didn't know was stolen, a lot of my life had been stolen as well.

God and I talked a lot about that. One of the conclusions I reached was that God had used this situation both to get my attention and to protect me. Remember my friend who was shot up on the street? That could have been me. The worst of the street violence in Benton Harbor broke out while I was in prison the first time, and a lot of my friends died in it. If I had been on the streets, I might have been killed too. Back in the nineties, Benton Harbor had more murders per capita than any place in the country.*

On my return to prison I got very involved with chapel. The guys there are broken before God, and I realized that's how God wants us to be with him. He needs us to be broken. As serious as I was about God, I still pretty much left

---

* Kotlowitz, *Other Side of the River*, 101.

him behind when I got out again after another year. Altogether I had served three full years for going for a ride with my friends who had stolen a car. I was twenty years old.

Once I got out I went to work. I found a job in a factory as a pot tender pouring molten metal into molds. It was a pretty good job. I worked there until 2005 when I went to work for a friend of mine at his full-service car wash. A couple of months later he started talking about how I needed my own shop. He'd already started looking for a second location and had found a place in Michigan City, Indiana, about forty miles from Benton Harbor. We worked out a deal where he helped with the financing to get me off the ground and the two locations shared a name. But the Michigan City location was to be all mine. We found the perfect site next to a gas station. I opened for a trial run toward the end of the season and the business took off. We closed for the season when the weather turned bad, with plans to open permanently the following March.

When I was growing up, my grandma and my dad taught me the value of work. My grandma had Jamal and me out picking blueberries in the fields and that sort of thing from as far back as I could remember. I always worked. Now that I had a chance to build a business of my own, I worked it as hard as I could. Most days I worked twelve hours, sometimes more. I ran specials and offered pick-up and delivery services for people's cars. I even did some late-night service so that guys who were getting ready to hang out with their friends could come through and have their cars detailed. I loved the work. I knew the location was going to be a hit. When the weather turned, which it does pretty early next to Lake Michigan, we started working on the paperwork to hit the ground running in the spring of 2006.

I loved my work, but my girlfriend did not. We started dating in 2003 and moved in together a little after that. As a Christian, I knew this wasn't right, but since I had left any thoughts of God back in the prison, I did it anyway. I thought we would eventually get married, especially after we found out she was pregnant, but my long hours working created a lot of problems for the two of us. I tried to explain why I worked so much and how I wanted to provide a good life for us and our baby, but the relationship fell apart.

As I mentioned earlier, my girlfriend moved out before she had the baby, and I didn't hear from her until the day she called my brother to say she was going to bring my son over to see me. That's why I went to the store, where I was arrested, and how I ended up back in jail, even though I had not done anything wrong. I didn't know anything about anyone's dope. The worst thing I had done was let Will use my cell phone.

After they arrested the two of us, I found out Will's name wasn't even Will. That was his street name, short for his last name, Williams. He could have cleared this whole thing up by telling the cops that it was his dope, not mine, but I knew he wasn't going to do that. If he did, he'd put himself in line to go to prison for a long time. Now that jail time was hanging over me.

I kept thinking this whole thing was going to go away. First, there wasn't any evidence against me. All they had was my phone, and if this drug sale had been set up in advance by phone, the cops had to see that I didn't make any calls to anyone connected to any of this mess prior to the one call Will made on my phone while I was in the store.

Speaking of the store, Will had parked his Durango right in front of an outdoor security camera. All they had to do was look at the tape and they would see me get out of the passenger side and walk into the store. They would also see Will get out and walk around to the passenger side and get in. I was so sure the tape would prove I was innocent that I asked my aunt, who came to see me, to go to the cops and make sure they looked at that tape.

But the biggest piece of evidence that I knew was going to set me free was the police report itself. They brought me a copy while I was in a cell, waiting to make bail. When I read the first line I thought, *Boom, that's it, I'm good to go because they have the wrong guy.* The report named Ox as the defendant, not me. I'm not Ox. I'm Zookie. I know Ox because he is my cousin (I have a lot of cousins), but I hardly ever saw him because he had moved to Atlanta a couple of years earlier. I didn't know why the police thought I was Ox or whether or not he had anything to do with drugs in Benton Harbor. It wasn't like we were close or anything. We saw each other maybe once every few years. I didn't know anything about his business, and I didn't want to know anything about his business. What he did or did not do was up to him.

I didn't bother reading the entire report. I didn't have to. The first line was enough to give me real hope that this was all going to just go away. The moment they realized I wasn't Ox, I'd go free.

I wasn't even worried about it. I knew I was innocent, and all the evidence proved it. That should have been enough. After all, in America aren't you supposed to be innocent until proven guilty?

4

TWO PLUS TWO EQUALS FOUR

Andrew

A couple of days after I arrested the man I thought was Ox, an FBI agent called my cell phone. I knew the FBI was working on an indictment for Ox on federal drug charges, which was going to be a great career booster for me. Anytime a small-town cop, like me, makes a big enough bust to get on the FBI's radar, everybody takes notice. It felt pretty good and created quite a buzz at the station.

I picked up the phone, a little nervous, a little excited. And then the agent asked, "Do you know you didn't get Ox?"

"I didn't?" I said very nonchalantly, trying to play it cool.

"No. You got his cousin, Zookie."

"Huh," I said as calm as I could while my mind raced, trying to come up with an answer to the question I knew he was going to ask next.

"But in your police report you wrote that you got Ox. So what happened?" the agent asked.

"Well, you know how it is. There are so many street names out there it's hard to keep them all straight. I just got them confused," I said.

"Okay, well, I need to get all the facts straight for this indictment. Did your informant tell you that you were looking for Ox or did he tell you that you were looking for Zookie?"

Without missing a beat I lied and said, "He told me I was looking for Zookie. I just messed it up in the report."

"All right. I need you to amend the original report to reflect that you were looking for Zookie, not Ox. This happens all the time. It's not a big deal. Once you have the amended report, send a copy over to me," the agent said.

"Sure. No problem," I said.

I hung up the phone and pulled up the original report I had filed. I could not just change the names. The report had already been submitted. Prosecutors and judges had already read the original report. Following police procedure, I added an amendment at the end stating that I meant to use the name Zookie, not Ox. Jameel McGee replaced Anthony R. as the drug dealer I was looking for when I went to the store on Fair Street. Then I signed the amendment, filed it, and sent a copy to the FBI agent working on the federal indictment. The amended report was filed two days after I had arrested Zookie.

Was the amendment a lie? Absolutely. Did I feel bad about it? Not for a minute, not then at least. I didn't care what the guy's name was. I found a softball-sized rock of crack cocaine that belonged to him. Sure, the car clearly belonged to the other guy, but I didn't give that a lot of thought. The bottom line was I had made a good bust. I wasn't about to let it fall apart. The whole question of guilt or innocence was settled in my mind the moment I found the dope in the cup holder. I didn't really care if the guy it belonged to was named Ox or Zookie or Mickey Mouse. I'd caught him in the act. Case closed. One more drug dealer off the street.

Amending the arrest report didn't present any more of a deep ethical dilemma than the way I had changed some of the details of the arrest in the first report.

It wasn't like this was the only time I wrote a police report to reflect what the prosecutor needed to hear rather than the facts of the case. When I was still a fairly new narcotics officer, I was involved in an operation with the local FBI office. Two federal officers chased a man into a liquor store, where they wrestled him to the ground. The man had thrown off a jacket as he sprinted into the store. After the arrest the officers searched the jacket and found a small amount of crack cocaine in one of the pockets. I arrived as the two officers led the suspect out of the store. One of them looked over at me. "We need you to write the report for us," he said.

I laughed. "I didn't see what happened."

"Do you know how to write a report?" he snapped back.

"Uh, yeah," I stammered.

"Good. This is now your suspect and your case. Thanks for taking care of the report for us," he said. They transferred the prisoner over to me and left. I wrote up the police report as if I had been right there with them as they made the bust. I felt a little funny doing it, but they had caught the suspect red handed. Who was I to question the methods of the FBI?

I had a similar experience on a bust with a Drug Enforcement Administration (DEA) agent. My partner and I went into an apartment with the agent. We had legal access to the residence because the renters of the apartment let us in. While my partner and I were conducting a protective sweep of the apartment to make sure there were no potential threats inside, the DEA agent began searching the residence without consent. Under a pile of clothes on a computer stand in the living room he discovered close to eight ounces of crack cocaine, which is a *lot* of crack.

There was just one problem with the bust: the search was a clear violation of the suspect's constitutional rights protecting him against illegal search and seizure. We didn't have consent or a warrant to conduct a search. The renters allowed us into the apartment only to come in and talk. Once inside we told them we needed to search for other people, which they said was okay. We heard a lot of noises coming from the back bedroom, which gave us reason to be cautious. But we never asked for permission to search for drugs. Now this huge bust was about to come apart because of what we saw as a technicality. After all, if we had taken the time to get a warrant, the crack might have disappeared before we could find it.

Rather than withdraw the arrest, the DEA agent coached me as I filled out the police report on the bust. I said the crack was in plain view when we entered the apartment. Because it was right out in the open, no search warrant was needed. I said we just glanced toward the computer table and the crack was right there for anyone to see. Thanks to the report, the suspect was indicted on federal drug charges.

Shaping the truth to ensure an indictment was something I learned was a necessary part of police work. In my mind, we had to do it. I came to believe all the legal advantages went to the drug dealers rather than law enforcement. Not long after I started at the Benton Harbor Police Department, a sergeant in the Berrien County narcotics unit explained it to me like this:

> Two plus two equals four. If you know someone is selling drugs and they run from you and when you catch them all you can find on them is a cell phone and a pocket full of cash in small denominations, you can deduce that they had drugs on them at some point with intent to distribute. If you walk back and retrace your path and find a baggie full of dope, you know it was his. You don't have to have seen him drop the dope to say that you saw him do it. *Two plus two equals four.* I also know that if you don't say you saw him drop it, you will not likely get a conviction. Therefore, you say what you need to say to make sure the bad guys are taken off the streets.

Two plus two equals four applied to a lot more than foot chases. I overheard a county sheriff's department senior narcotics officer bragging about how he always got consent to enter a residence where he suspected drugs were being sold. "I just have a couple of officers go around back. When I knock on the front door they yell, 'Come in.' How am I supposed to know it wasn't the people in the house inviting me in?" he said with a smile.

This same officer used an equally effective technique to get consent for searches without a warrant from the Hispanic community in our area. He'd ask someone if they spoke English. When they told him, "No," he'd nod his head and smile in agreement. More often than not, whomever he wanted to search would smile and nod too. This officer then claimed the nod was a visible consent to the search. Few ever put up a fight at the scene when he started searching a residence or vehicle. Many of the Spanish-speaking population with whom we dealt in our area were afraid of the police and never objected as their rights were violated. Claims from an officer that they nodded and gave consent always held up in court. I learned pretty fast that prosecutors, judges, and juries usually, if not always, believe the testimony of a law-enforcement officer over the word of a drug dealer.

Defense attorneys were also swayed by the testimony of a police officer, even when they knew things were not always as they appeared. I had an interesting conversation with a defense attorney after one case. We ended up in the elevator of the courthouse together, just the two of us. He turned to me and said, "I know how this works." I smiled and told him I didn't know what he was talking about. He went on to assure me that he golfs with a lot of police officers and they share that sometimes it's necessary to lie under oath to get the job done. I almost let my guard down but instead responded, "That's terrible they do that." My smile probably betrayed my words.

Once I learned how to bend the rules, I found it easier to do my job. Not long after I started at the department, I expressed frustration to a fellow officer because I just knew a car had drugs in it but I had no reason to pull it over. This conversation took place during the winter. Since Benton Harbor sits on the shores of Lake Michigan, we get a lot of lake-effect snow. Little did I know that snow can be a very helpful tool for police work. My fellow officer told me how.

"You know, Collins, it's a violation to have snow built up on your license plate when it obstructs the view from vehicles behind it."

I sort of shrugged and said, "That won't do me any good. His plate was clear." I felt proud that I had been thorough enough to at least look for that violation.

The officer smiled and shook his head in disbelief. "Do you think the driver knew his plate wasn't covered?"

"No," I said, unsure of what he was saying to me. Then it hit me.

"When you pull the car over, walk around back and do a little sweep across the tag. That way the driver can't deny his plate was covered because he saw you clean it off. And while you have him pulled over, you might as well check the car for drugs."

Since we did not have in-car dash cameras, this tactic worked.

When spring rolled around and the snow stopped falling, I learned another trick. Michigan, like every state in the country, has a seat-belt law. However, sometimes it's hard to tell from behind whether or not a driver is wearing his or her seat belt. Seat-belt violations gave me a convenient excuse to pull over cars I suspected for drugs. When I walked up to the driver's-side window, I acted relieved that the driver was buckled up. Since I was such a fair officer, I did not give him a ticket for a seat-belt violation. However, I always needed to check the car to make sure there was nothing illegal inside. Before the driver knew what hit him, he was thanking me for not writing him a seat-belt ticket while I transported him to jail for the drugs I found after the illegal stop.

Finding probable cause to search a car wasn't nearly as difficult as I initially thought. A more experienced officer from a different department told me the magic words that always justify a search: "I thought I smelled marijuana." I also became an eagle eye at spotting possible marijuana seeds on a car floorboard or on the upholstery. No judge ever threw out a vehicle search conducted because of a possible marijuana seed. I felt very confident using these methods because older officers as well as officers from other departments and agencies did the same thing. I also justified my actions by telling myself I was taking drugs and drug dealers off the street. With time, I started gaining a reputation for being a hard-nosed cop that drug dealers didn't want to mess with. I loved that reputation.

I do not want you to think my work as a cop was what caused me to com-promise my integrity. Long before I could even find Benton Harbor on a map, I had already compromised that part of my life. When I was growing up, my situation was a little different from most of the guys I knew. My mom was only fifteen when she had me. I didn't meet my biological father until I was twelve. Because my mom was so young, there were times she was more like a sister to me than a mother. We lived next door to my grandparents, who provided the stability I did not always get at home. Their house was my safe haven. They took me to church, and when I was seven I gave my life to Christ. But I didn't exactly live what I said I believed.

My mom and stepdad smoked and drank, so I tried both. I started smok-ing when I was a young teenager. I could say my mom didn't care, which isn't exactly true. I'm sure she cared, but her philosophy was that if I was going to do something, she preferred I do it in front of her instead of hiding it. My grand-parents, however, were another story. It wasn't so much that they forbid smok-ing. I knew they didn't like it, but there was more to it than that. I didn't want them to know that I smoked, because I knew how much it hurt them that my mother smoked. I did not want to disappoint them too.

One day I had been smoking at a friend's house and then went to my grandparents' house. Before I got there, I chewed a piece of gum and did all the other little tricks smokers do to try to get rid of the smell. I went into the kitchen and started talking with my grandmother. At one point she said, "Honey, why do you smoke?"

"Why do I smoke?" I said, a little panicked. "I don't smoke."

"I can smell it on you," she said.

"Oh, I was over at David's house, and his parents smoke, so it must be on my clothes," I lied, trying to cover my tracks.

"His parents smoke, huh? Did they blow it right into your mouth? I can smell it on your breath."

I dropped my head, ashamed, trying to think of the next thing to say, try-ing to find another excuse rather than own up to what I had done. My grand-mother didn't let me hang there long. "Would you like a snack?" she asked, and we never talked about my smoking again. She didn't need to mention it because she had already said enough.

Eventually I quit smoking, but not for a while. It's tough to smoke when you aren't old enough to buy cigarettes. However, I found an answer to that. My grandfather made deliveries to stores for Little Debbie snack cakes. I used to help him empty the product out of the cardboard boxes and place it onto store shelves. When the box was empty, he always smashed it flat. I was once in a store with him, emptying boxes, when I spotted some cigarettes on a shelf near the one on which I worked. When no one was looking, I swept several packs into the box I had just emptied, then volunteered to take it outside and smash it.

My petty larceny aside, I also lied just to get attention from people. There were times I heard someone tell a really great story about themselves or one of their family members, and I turned around and told the same story about myself. I don't know why I did it. For attention, I guess. That is why my entire high school graduating class thought I was color-blind.

In ninth grade our science teacher was talking about color blindness, and he asked if anyone in the class was color-blind. One kid raised his hand. When I saw the outpouring of sympathy toward him by everyone else in the class, I raised my hand too. That little lie followed me until the day I left my hometown and moved to Benton Harbor. All my friends thought I really was color-blind.

My grandparents even got to where they believed it. And one day some of my friends were over at my house, and they asked my mother if she had to pick out my socks since I was color-blind. She smiled and said, "No, he is really good about it. He manages."

I couldn't believe my ears. My mom knew the truth, but she didn't call me out on it. Later, after everyone had gone home, I asked her why. "Well, I figured I didn't want to bust you in front of your friends." Looking back, I think I would have been relieved if she had. When I went to the police academy, my friends and even some family members worried that I was going to flunk out because police officers can't be color-blind.

The fact that I had such a loose grasp on truthfulness growing up made it easier for me to adjust to certain methodologies in police work that weren't completely on the level. There was a big difference, though, in my mind. I lied about being color-blind to draw attention to myself. I played a little fast and loose with facts on my police reports and even in my court testimonies because I wanted to get bad guys off the streets. This wasn't about me, I convinced myself. This was about being a good cop and doing whatever had to be done to clean up Benton Harbor.

At least that's what I told myself.

The truth was, I broke the rules and outright lied on my reports because I loved the attention I got when I made a big bust and when an arrest resulted in someone's going off to prison. I was the youngest officer in the department and I was its rising star. The more arrests I made, the more my superiors noticed. The whole thing became a vicious circle. I was becoming an addict to the attention, to the adrenaline high of an arrest—to myself and my own ego.

That is why I had no trouble writing and amending Jameel's arrest report to reflect what the feds needed to bring an indictment against him. Not long after his arrest, I was doing a lot more than just making up facts on reports. I had already started planting the seeds of my own downfall.

5

INDICTED

Jameel

After spending three days in jail, I finally made bail. I still expected the whole thing to go away since they were after Ox, not me. When I got home I found out my ex had indeed come by with my baby son. After she heard I'd been arrested, she was long gone to Fort Wayne or Alabama or somewhere. She didn't want her baby around a drug dealer, because, of course, she assumed I was guilty. A lot of my friends and family assumed the same. Word on the street was that I'd been caught with the dope on me. No matter how loudly I claimed I was innocent, most people had trouble believing me, even those who knew me best. The police really needed to clear this up and fast.

I knew the best way to prove I was innocent was to get ahold of the security tape from outside the store where I'd been arrested. My aunt called the police and told them the tape could clear me. "If you can find evidence for your nephew, ma'am, then you need to secure it yourself," she was told.

My aunt then called the store. "I'm sorry but we cannot release the security tape to you," the manager said. "We can only turn it over to the police."

My aunt called the police again and told them what the manager had said. I don't know if she talked to Andrew or someone else. Whoever it was cut her off: "Your nephew shouldn't have been selling dope. Stop calling us." And they hung up.

I contacted my state court–appointed attorney and told him about the tape. He didn't really seem to care. Several weeks later when I finally got to meet with him, I discovered he'd also been appointed to defend Will, the guy driving the car who could have cleared this whole thing up. I actually overheard my attorney telling Will that if he testified against me, his charges would be reduced or dropped. I pretty much knew I was screwed when that happened.

Long before I overheard that conversation between my attorney and Will, I was out on bail and still hopeful that in spite of what the cops told my aunt, the police had to know they had the wrong guy. Once they figured that out, this whole thing would go away. In the meantime, I needed to make some money to pay back the people who came up with my bail money. I knew I could pay them back quickly when I opened my car wash, but that was still a few weeks away. The money thing really weighed on me.

For the first couple of days after I was released on bail, I just sort of laid low at my grandma's house. On the third day I got a call from one of my homies, Greg, who asked, "Hey, man. You still hook up music in cars?"

"Yeah."

"Well I need you to hook up my music real fast. I just got a new CD player I need you to put in."

"All right, cool," I said. "Where you at?"

"Over on Bus Street," he said and gave me his address.

"I'll be there quick," I said. I was glad to have something to do and a way to make a little money. I had some money on me when I was arrested, money they did not return to me when I was released on bail. Back in 2006 when all this went down, Michigan had a law that allowed police to seize and keep any money or property involved in criminal activity. Since they assumed I had been dealing drugs, they assumed the money I had in my pocket came from drug sales. It hadn't, but that didn't seem to matter to anyone but me.

When I arrived at Greg's house, I got right to work. I pulled the old radio out of his car and started to install the new one. Then I realized the electrical tape I needed was in the house, so I crawled out of the car to go inside. As I did, I noticed a car rolling slowly down the street. I recognized the driver. It was the cop who'd busted me less than a week before, Andrew Collins. "Hmm, what's that dude doing over here in an unmarked police car?" I said out loud to myself.

I went into the house and got all the stuff I needed to finish the job. When I walked back out, Greg stepped over to me and said, "That's a sheriff's car sitting right there."

I looked and saw a clearly marked squad car parked on the street. "Oh, wow. They must be fixing to arrest somebody," I said, then returned to the car to get back to work. With so many drug houses in Benton Harbor, seeing a patrol car parked on the street with cops about to raid a house is no big deal. Back then it was just life in my hometown. I knew they couldn't be looking for me since I had just been released on bail three days earlier, and I hadn't done anything anyway.

A few minutes after I crawled back in the car, I heard car doors slam. I looked up to see a couple of cops walking up Greg's driveway right toward me. I jumped out of the car and stood up.

"Jameel McGee," one of them said, "we have a warrant for your arrest."

"There ain't no way," I said and started walking away from the cops. "No man, there ain't no way. I ain't done *nothing* wrong. You got the wrong person. Leave me alone."

"Jameel McGee, you've been indicted on federal drug charges for possession with intent to distribute," the cop said. As he said this he pulled out his handcuffs.

"Look, man, I got no idea what you are talking about. You just leave me alone and get on somewhere so I can get back to work," I said. I was starting to get mad, which is why I was walking away from the cops.

"No, you're going to jail. Your indictment just came in. You need to come with us."

Now I was really about to lose it. "I'm indicted? Call it in. I need to hear it myself. Otherwise I ain't going nowhere with you." I'd already made up my mind I was not going to let them arrest me again for something I didn't do. But the cops kept moving closer and closer to me. "Don't get too close or we're going to have a problem," I said. And I meant it.

One of them pulled out his Taser. "Don't make me use this," he warned.

I stopped backing up. "Use it. If you're gonna use it, you use it right now, but that thing ain't going to be enough 'cause I'm going to pull those wires out and then I'm coming right at you."

I wasn't thinking about what might happen next. All the anger I felt about being arrested a week earlier, along with the anger I had bottled up inside me over the wrongful arrest and conviction back when I was fifteen, came boiling up. This wasn't going to end well, and at that point I really didn't care.

All of a sudden my brother Richard ran over and jumped in front of me and grabbed me by the shoulders. Greg had called him as soon as the police showed up.

"Zookie!" Richard yelled.

"What?"

"Zookie, calm down, man. You don't want to do this. Man, just go on down to the station. You ain't got nothing to worry about. Just go down there. You'll be good," Richard said.

I looked Richard in the eye. He looked scared, which sort of pulled me back.

"Okay, okay," I said. The cops just stood there, looking at me. "You know what? Forget it. I'm gonna go down there and get this over with 'cause I got stuff to do. I ain't got time to keep messing with this. Let's just get this mess over with once and for all."

Richard looked relieved. I was relieved too when a short time later, as I sat in a holding cell in the Benton Harbor police station, an FBI agent came over to me and said, "You're not Ox."

"No, I'm not," I said.

"What's your name?" he asked.

"Jameel McGee."

He didn't say anything. He just turned around and left.

"All righty then," I said and let out a sigh of relief. I truly believed this was finally going to be okay. Now they knew I was not the guy they were after. I waited for someone to come back to my cell and let me go home. In a perfect world they might also apologize for the mix-up, but I knew that was never going to happen. I didn't need an apology. I just wanted to go home and get on with my life. But nobody came back. Not the FBI agent. Not one Benton Harbor cop. Not Andrew Collins. No one. I sat there for three days, waiting.

Finally, someone showed up. They handed me a short stack of papers. I immediately knew what it was. They had to give me a copy of the arrest report and show me the charges filed against me. I saw the report was the same one I'd been given when I was arrested a few days earlier when this whole mess began. But this one was longer. Stapled to the original report was an amended version. As soon as I read the first line, I knew I was in trouble. Where the original had the name Anthony R. throughout, the amended version replaced every instance with Jameel McGee; Ox was now Zookie.

I was screwed. I started reading. The more I read the madder I felt. Nothing lined up with what had actually happened. The report, written by Andrew Collins, said he arrested me while I was inside the Durango. That was a lie. The security tape could easily have shown I was not in the car when the cops arrived, but I had my doubts that the tape even existed anymore. He also wrote in the report that I had leaned toward the center console before raising my hands. That was a huge lie. I was inside the store buying milk for my baby when the cops arrived. No one would believe me now, not when a cop said I was in the car with the dope.

God meant for me to be in that cell by myself when I read the report because if anyone had been with me I might have done something stupid. I was depressed and angrier than I had ever been in my life, and I just needed to vent. It didn't help that the bailiffs and everyone else I'd dealt with while I was being booked said something about how I faced a federal indictment and the feds don't indict unless they know they can get a conviction. Most people do not realize the feds have nearly a 99 percent conviction rate on cases like the one I faced. Everyone connected to my case had already made up their mind that I was guilty, including the state court–appointed attorney I had in Benton Harbor.

I also had a probation officer from an earlier case where my brother had bought himself a gun on the streets for protection after someone had stabbed him. I was in the car with my brother when he got pulled over. To protect my brother, I said the gun was mine. I received probation for suspicion of carrying a concealed weapon, which I shouldn't have because you can't be convicted of being suspected of doing something. You either did it or you didn't. But I got probation anyway. Now that I had been arrested again for something I didn't do, my probation officer pretty much yelled at me, "You're so stupid for doing this! You're a father now. What is wrong with you?"

"But I didn't have anything to do with this," I replied.

"Yeah, right," she huffed and walked out on me.

Right then I knew no one was going to listen to me. There was nothing I could do to change this situation outside of a miracle, or someone in the police department actually looking at evidence like the security tape from the store. But I knew that wasn't going to happen.

A few days after I read the amended police report, two officers came to my cell.

"Jameel?" one said.

"Yep," I replied.

"I'm Officer Lange and this is Officer Modigell. We're going to transport you to the federal justice building in Grand Rapids."

"Now?" I asked.

"Right now." I was then placed in shackles, with my hands and feet cuffed and a chain in front of me connecting them. Officers Lange and Modigell then led me out to an unmarked car. They walked. I sort of shuffled along. People stared at me as I went by, which made me feel like less than a man and more like an animal on display. I think that was the point of shackling me. It's not like I was a dangerous criminal who might try to escape or hurt someone.

The drive from Benton Harbor to Grand Rapids takes a little under an hour and a half. It was a long hour and a half for me. As soon as we got in the car, Officers Lange and Modigell started trying to pump me for information. They first read me my Miranda rights and then started in.

"You know you're doing ten years in prison," Lange said. "There's no way around it."

I didn't say anything.

"No," he continued, "you aren't coming home, not for a long time. You're staring at a ten-year sentence, minimum."

I tried to ignore him.

"Yep. Ten years. Your only hope to get that reduced is to give us some information."

"You need some information, do ya?" I finally replied.

Lange looked over at Modigell and smiled. "Yeah, we need some information. You got something for us?"

"Y'all already got all the information you need, but y'all misusing it," I said.

Lange gave a sarcastic laugh. "Oh. And just how are we misusing it?"

"Because you know this is not my case and you know those were not my drugs and you know I ain't got nothing to do with none of this," I said. "I was just riding with that guy to get milk for my baby. Y'all know that wasn't my car and it wasn't my dope . . . and you know I didn't do nothing."

Modigell spoke up. "Oh yeah," he said with a "gotcha" tone of voice. "Well, we talked to Williams and he said you were involved. We talked to everybody, and everybody said you did this. They told us everything you've done."

I shook my head in disbelief. "Prove it," I said.

Lange jumped in. "No. It's your job to prove it."

"Yeah, man, you're right. It's my job to prove I'm innocent."

I already knew that. I had learned it the hard way when I was fifteen. The

Constitution of the United States might say you're innocent until proven guilty, but that's not how it is on the streets. If you get arrested, you're guilty unless you can prove otherwise. And if the cops insist they saw you do whatever they claim to have caught you doing, you might as well give up. There's nothing you can do. I guess if you're rich, you can hire a really good lawyer and have him get to work finding evidence to take apart the prosecutor's case, but there aren't many people out there who can afford to do that. The rest of us, like I said, are screwed.

"Oh yeah," one of the officers in the front seat said, "you're going to get ten years." He sounded really happy about it.

"I ain't got nothing else to say," I said. For the rest of the drive I just sat in the back seat and stared out the window. Lange and Modigell kept trying to get me to say something. They asked me questions about who else I knew was dealing drugs in town, and they asked a lot of questions about my cousin Ox. When I didn't reply, they got mad, but I just sat there, mute.

When we finally arrived at the Grand Rapids federal justice building, they pulled me out of the car and led me to the processing desk. The officer in charge asked me my name. I did not reply. He asked my date of birth. I kept my mouth shut. He asked my Social Security number. I did not say a word. He asked me my name again.

I looked at him and said, "Get it from them," and nodded toward Lange and Modigell. At this point I'd cooperated about as much as I felt like cooperating.

Lange answered all the questions for me. I stood there as the processing officer filled out his forms. Once they were finished, Lange and Modigell turned to leave. As they did, Lange said, "See you in ten years." Modigell chuckled and they walked away.

I did not see them again until my trial, where Lange had all sorts of stories to tell about me.

The entire time I was in the Benton Harbor jail I'd worn my street clothes. Now the first thing they did in Grand Rapids was order me to strip. Everything came off. Once I was completely naked, an officer said, "Bend over." I did as I was told. "Squat." I complied. "Cough." I coughed. "All right, turn around. Raise your sac." I lifted my testicles to show I wasn't hiding any drugs or weapons.

Keep in mind, I had also been strip-searched when I was booked in Benton Harbor. I never left my cell and never had contact with another human being except the two officers who drove me to Grand Rapids. Still, I was strip-searched when I arrived at the federal justice building in Grand Rapids. It was the first of many searches I went through. Every prisoner is strip-searched whenever he moves from one facility to another.

To me, the whole thing seemed to be about dehumanizing me and making sure I understood that I was nothing in this world and nothing in my community and nothing to anybody. It's a hard lesson to miss.

The whole time this was taking place I kept shaking my head in disbelief. One of the officers said something like, "What's wrong with you?"

"Man, I didn't do this. I had nothing to do with it. I'm innocent."

The officers in the room snickered and laughed. I kept my mouth shut after that. Finally I was taken to a cell and locked up. Unlike the day I was arrested while working on my buddy's car, I already knew how this was going to turn out, and it wasn't going to be good for me. I sank down on my bunk, depressed. Surely the people who put me here knew I was innocent. Why would they do this to me? What had I ever done to deserve this?

6

INTO THE ABYSS

Andrew

About a year before I arrested Jameel, I was out on patrol on a cold, snowy day when a call for officer assistance came over my radio. I flipped on my lights and siren and headed toward the south end of Benton Harbor. Eventually I found the car of the county narcotics officer who had radioed for help. The man was a living legend in the area. Dealers I'd arrested said when the Legend came to town, it was time to close up shop until his shift was over. That was the reputation I wanted. I tried to learn everything I could from him.

When I pulled up to the scene, the Legend walked out from behind a house red faced, out of breath, and angry.

"Anthony got away—*right here*!" he shouted.

Right here was a snow-covered alley. A set of footprints led down the alley from a new Chevy, the motor still running and the driver's door open. I recognized the name Anthony. Everyone in town knew he was a heroin dealer. I'd questioned him a few times and had good rapport with him.

The Legend went on, "I pulled him over because I

knew his license was no good. When I walked up to his car, the guy punched it and took off. I chased him here, but he got away on foot. I know he has drugs on him. The guy never runs unless he's carrying."

"I'll search the car," I said.

The Legend took off, following the footprints down the alley. At this point in my career I didn't have a lot of experience, but I knew how to search a vehicle systematically. We called it "tossing" a car, which means exactly what it sounds like. When you toss a car, you tear out everything, and I mean everything.

Right off I knew this Chevy had to be a rental because it was the cleanest car I'd ever seen. Drug dealers often use rentals to do business. They'll have a girlfriend or relative rent the vehicle so it can't be traced back to them. If they flee from the police in a rental, there is no paper trail. Dealers also prefer rentals because it keeps police from seeing them using the same vehicle week after week, something that is pretty easy to notice in a small town like Benton Harbor. The fact this was a rental car didn't stop me from making a mess of it. I even tore out the back seat, looking for drugs or weapons. I didn't find a thing.

After I searched the car, I heard on the dispatcher radio that they'd discovered footprints leading to a house. I jumped in my car and drove to the location. The Legend and some other officers were already there. As we started to search the house, I heard a bloodcurdling scream from behind. I spun around to see a female officer with her gun drawn, pointing toward a backyard shed.

"He's in there," she yelled. "I opened the door and he was right there, looking back at me."

Officers descended on the shed. I went with them. When I stepped inside, I spotted Anthony hiding behind some junk in a corner. He knew me, which made this part a lot easier.

"Come on out, man. You're caught," I said.

Anthony threw his arms in the air. The look on his face was sheer terror.

"Collins, man, don't let that dude whip me," he pleaded.

"I won't, man. Come on out," I said.

When he stepped out, the Legend and another county officer rushed past me, tackled Anthony, and threw him to the ground, all the while screaming at him to stop resisting. One of the officers kicked Anthony in the side after he'd been handcuffed. He told Anthony that's what he got for running. I felt sorry for Anthony, but I didn't speak up. There's an unwritten code that you always protect your fellow officers. I wasn't going to break that code for a heroin dealer.

Eventually I hauled Anthony up off the ground and to my patrol car.

Over and over he asked me, "Why, Collins, why'd they have to do that, man?"

I didn't have an answer. I tried to assure him nothing else was going to happen to him as long as he cooperated. I doubt he believed me, not that I could blame him.

After securing Anthony in the back seat of my patrol car, I drove to the alley where Anthony had dumped the rental car. While I sat in my car with Anthony, I watched the Legend and the county officer who had kicked Anthony go back and search his car. It seemed like a waste of time. I had already tossed it pretty good, but these two took tossing to a completely different level. They absolutely destroyed the car. The more they searched, the madder the Legend became because the car was clean.

Finally, the two officers went to the trunk of the Legend's car and stood talking for a couple of moments. Then the Legend pulled something out of his trunk. I couldn't believe my eyes when I saw what appeared to be a plastic baggie filled with what looked like marijuana.

Anthony saw it too. "They gonna plant something in my car. I know they is," he shouted.

"Relax, you have nothing to worry about. I'll check it out," I said.

I went over to the Legend as he exited Anthony's car. He smiled at me and waved the baggie of marijuana in the air.

"At least now I know he'll get strip-searched when he gets to the county lockup," he said.

And that is exactly what happened to Anthony. He was booked for possession of marijuana. I learned that day that if a suspect was brought in for a drug-related offense, they were routinely strip-searched to protect the jail from contraband. Anthony was not found with any "additional" drugs, and the drug charges were dropped after he pleaded guilty to fleeing and eluding. But that confession sent Anthony off to prison.

After watching what happened to Anthony, I promised myself I would never plant evidence. The Legend may have carried a supply of dope in his trunk to give a boost to a weak case, but I wasn't going to do that. I told myself I had too much integrity to stoop that low. I soon discovered, however, that once you cross the line and play fast and loose with the truth, there are no rules you won't break, not even the ones you set for yourself.

I kept that promise, sort of. I did not carry drugs in my patrol car on a regular basis. Once I became a full-time narcotics officer, though, that promise to myself disappeared. I kept a stash of dope in a purple Crown Royal bag in my office at the station. I never planned on collecting drugs that I could use as evidence in a weak case. The whole thing started pretty much by accident and laziness.

One afternoon, not long after I became a narcotics officer, I stopped a group of teenagers I knew had some dope. When I pulled up, they all sort of froze. "Where's the dope?" I asked, and they melted. They all knew they were about to go to jail for possession. I could have taken them in, but these weren't the kind of offenders I was after. These kids were customers, not dealers. I made them surrender their bag of marijuana and sent them home with a stern warning.

When I got back to the station that night, I should have processed the pot and written up a report, but the report would have raised a lot of needless questions. The way I saw it, no one expected me to bring in some kids with a bag of pot they'd pooled their money to buy. Writing a report wasn't worth the hassle for me, them, or anyone. But if I didn't write the report, how was I to explain the bag of pot I'd taken from them? I didn't want to think too much about that question. Instead, I tossed the pot into my duty bag and sort of forgot about it.

Over time I made more stops like this, where I caught guys with dope and didn't run them in. I confiscated their drugs and let them off with a warning. I started to collect so much dope that I stopped carrying it in my patrol bag and switched to a Crown Royal bag. My bag started to fill up, and it didn't take long for me to find a use for it. Honestly, I felt I had to.

In the middle of winter during my second year on the force, I pulled up to a known drug house in a known drug area and saw two guys standing in front of the house near an electrical box. The weather was so cold that no one would be standing around outside for their health. Another officer was with me, and we approached the two guys. As we got close to them, they took off in opposite directions. I caught up to my suspect, wrestled him down, and frisked him for drugs or weapons. My partner caught the other. Both men had large amounts of money in small bills with no explanation for it, along with cell phones that kept ringing. Both the small bills and incessantly ringing cell phones screamed drug dealer.

I walked back to the electrical box where the men had been standing. When I opened it, I discovered a large amount of individually packaged bags of crack cocaine. Immediately I arrested the men for possession of crack with intent to distribute.

To me, this looked like an open-and-shut case. The prosecutor, however, was very cautious after I told her I had not seen either defendant touch or move toward the electrical box. (Obviously, this took place before I arrested Jameel McGee.)

"Are you sure you didn't see any furtive gestures when they were moving away from that electrical box?" she asked me.

"No, I didn't," I replied.

She sighed. "This is going to be a tough case now. I wish you had seen them touching that box. That would make this case much easier," she said.

Fast-forward a year or so. I stopped the car of a known drug dealer. I'd been after him for a while. When I approached the car, the smell of marijuana was very strong. The defendant climbed out, but he was less than cooperative. A big, boisterous guy, he threw a fit about being pulled over. When I patted him down, I found what looked like marijuana seeds in his pocket. The man was also driving without a license. I booked him for possession, but that was going to be a hard case to make since I'd found only seeds on him.

An idea popped into my head. I went back to my office and removed a baggie of the pot I'd stashed in my purple Crown Royal bag and added it to the evidence from the arrest. Since I smelled pot in the car and found seeds in his pocket, supplementing the evidence I needed to make my case did not seem like a big deal. The guy was guilty. I just helped the case along a little. At least that's what I told myself.

Later on I used my stash of drugs to help myself out financially. I didn't sell them. I would never do that. But as a narcotics officer I often made what is called a controlled buy from an informant. On a controlled buy, money was given to a confidential informant to buy drugs at a specific location. Once the snitch brought back the drugs and provided a brief description of the inside of the house, we paid him for his service. The going rate was ten dollars to buy the drugs and twenty to thirty dollars for the actual service. I was paying upward of fifty dollars for a ten-dollar rock. This, of course, was a ten-dollar rock before the informant cut off a small amount prior to meeting me at the rendezvous point.

One Friday night I was in my office, feeling down and unappreciated. I had recently gotten married and had promised to take my wife out on a date, but I was broke. Benton Harbor is a small police department, and my pay reflected that. This Friday night I was flat broke, and payday didn't roll around until the following Wednesday. This did not seem fair.

During my time as a police officer, Michigan had a civil forfeiture law, as do many other states. The law allows the government to take cash, cars, homes, and other property suspected of being involved in criminal activity. *Suspected* is the key word. When I busted someone for drugs, the city of Benton Harbor confiscated any cash we found on the suspect, as well as the car the suspect was driving and even his house if we believed it was a key part of his drug business.

All charges could eventually be dismissed or the suspect could be found not guilty, but he didn't get his property back. Instead, the money and property rolled into the local police department and city government. Part of the money could also go to repay crime victims, but not in narcotics, the world in which I worked. All the money went to the department. Part of it went into the narcotics fund, which was supposed to finance our part in the war on drugs, and a lot of it just went into a general fund.

Because I made more drug arrests than anyone else, and because I was one of the most aggressive officers in the department, I brought in a lot of money to the city and the police department. Even so, my pay was so low I couldn't afford to take my new bride out to dinner on a Friday night.

The more I thought about all this, the angrier I became. *I bring in tens of thousands of dollars to the police department, but they don't have the decency to pay me enough to take my wife out on a date!* At no time did I consider the fact that I had mismanaged my money and put myself in the position of being broke before payday. That thought never crossed my mind. Instead, I stewed on the injustice of it all until I convinced myself the department owed me big. And now it was time for them to start making things right.

Rather than march into the chief's office and ask for a raise, I wrote a report describing a controlled buy from an informant who didn't know I was using his name. I turned in the report along with a baggie of dope from my stash. The department then "reimbursed" me to the tune of forty dollars, and I had enough money to take my wife out to dinner. To me, this wasn't stealing because the money came out of the money I'd brought in through civil forfeitures. When I put the money in my pocket, I didn't feel guilty because I'd convinced myself I'd earned it.

I "earned" several more "reimbursements" over the next few months. Because I made so many legitimate arrests, no one questioned these fake reports and no one audited my books. After all, I had the drugs to go with the report, which meant no one had a reason to suspect a thing.

Later in my police career I figured out another way to make a little extra cash from the narcotics fund. The department started a new program where we paid informants $500 if the information they gave us resulted not only in an arrest but also in a gun coming off the streets. It was a good policy, and I found a way to make it even better for me.

The idea came to me one day while I was conducting a search with a warrant I'd secured without any information from an informant. The case involved drugs, but I also found a handgun in the suspect's possession. A light bulb went on. When I got back to the station to write up my report, I added the name of an informant who'd supposedly provided the information. The name was real, but the information was not. Again, the informant had no idea I was using his name. Since the department paid informants in cash and I was supposed to deliver it to him, I simply pocketed the $500. The informant had to sign a receipt for the money, but that was an easy fix. I just scribbled his name on the line and turned it into my superiors. No one questioned what I was doing nor did I think too much of taking the money, because, again, I had convinced myself that I had earned it. I brought so much money into the department that I deserved to have a little of it come my way.

Taking money from the narcotics fund, which I helped build up, was one thing, but I told myself I would never take money from a drug dealer's pocket. Whatever money I found while making a bust I gave to the department. I wasn't being entirely altruistic. As our narcotics team brought more and more money into the department, we were given more freedom to do our jobs, no questions asked. And I really wanted that freedom.

Every day I became more and more aggressive in the way I carried out my job. If I bent the rules a little, no one seemed to mind. And if I skimmed a little walking-around money for myself, what did that matter as long as I pulled bad guys off the streets, along with the money and property they forfeited to the city?

With time, the money I personally brought in through civil forfeitures topped $50,000 a year, and this in a city that covers a mere four square miles. I had to file a report with the state of Michigan every year, describing how much money was forfeited because of this law. The police department then posted stats every month showing how much each officer had brought in through civil forfeiture. Whenever the new stat sheet went up, officers gathered round, comparing who did better in what category. Seeing how incredible my forfeiture totals were compared to the others' fed my ego. For me, this scorecard proved I was the star of the department, the indispensable narcotics officer this little town was lucky to have. Not only was I a great police officer, but I even paid my own way. The honest taxpaying citizens of Benton Harbor received my incredible services free of charge because I brought in far more money than it cost to employ me.

Friedrich Nietzsche wrote, "He who fights with monsters should be careful lest he thereby become a monster. And if thou gaze long into an abyss, the abyss will also gaze into thee."* I did not realize how deeply the abyss had looked into me. I had become a monster, not out of greed or zeal or my questionable tactics or lack of integrity. No, I fell into the abyss because I was weighed down by pride. Proverbs 16:18 says, "Pride goes before destruction, a haughty spirit before a fall." I didn't know it at the time, but these words were about to come true in my life in a very painful and public way.

---

* Friedrich Nietzsche, *Beyond Good and Evil* (New York: Macmillan, 1907), 97.

7

GUILTY UNTIL
PROVEN INNOCENT

Jameel

As soon as I was processed at the federal detention center in Grand Rapids, I had to appear before a judge to enter a plea to the charges of possession of crack cocaine with intent to distribute. Two minutes before I walked into the courtroom, I met my federal court–ordered attorney, John Karafa, for the first time.

"How are you pleading?" John asked me.

"Not guilty," I said.

"All right," he said. We then walked into the courtroom to appear before the magistrate. The judge read the charges against me and asked how I was pleading.

"Not guilty, your honor," John said.

The judge did not react one way or another. He simply stated, "In the matter of a bond, are you prepared, Mr. Karafa, to proceed with a bond hearing?"

"We request the bond hearing be delayed two days until I have sufficient time to consult with my client," John replied.

The magistrate said, "Very well, then. Bond hearing is set for two days. Next case."

Two days later we appeared before the same magistrate. He set my bond and let me leave the federal detention center after posting bail. Even though I was officially out on bail, I could not return home. The court sent me to a facility in Benton Harbor called KPEP, which stands for Kalamazoo Probation Enhancement Program. The program started in Kalamazoo but now covers the entire state of Michigan. KPEP is basically a halfway house to help those leaving prison transition back into society. It does career training and helps you find a job. At the time, the Benton Harbor KPEP program was housed in the old Mercy Hospital, which was where I was born. The town has since torn the building down.

I was not happy about being sent to KPEP. For one thing, it's a halfway house for people *getting out of prison*. I was out on bail and facing serious jail time for something I didn't do. Everyone in KPEP has already been convicted of their crimes, and that's how they looked at me. I don't mean they treated me badly. I mean no one there believed me when I said I was innocent.

While at KPEP I was also supposed to find a job. I could leave during the day to go job hunting, but I had to be back at a certain time and spend my nights there. My counselors kept after me to find a job, but I didn't see much point in it. I figured finding a job was a waste of time because if they found me guilty, I obviously wasn't going to be coming back to that job anytime soon. And if they found me not guilty, I'd leave that job because I had a car wash to get off the ground. Even so, every day I was reminded that I needed to find a job. They also wanted me to cut my hair, which I wasn't going to do either.

The main reason I hated KPEP was the fact that the place reminded me of the BS charges against me and how I wasn't even supposed to be there. I hated it. Every day my attitude got a little worse. I felt myself starting to become the person the cops and prosecutors said I was. Those close to me were starting to believe it too. When the federal indictment came down, even some of my own family believed I was guilty.

My attorney came to see me once while I was at KPEP to go over my case. We talked about the charges, but we mainly talked about the tape from the store that could prove I was innocent. Collins said in the police report that he arrested me while I was sitting in Will's Durango. That was a lie. I got out of the car and went right into the store. If we could just get ahold of that tape, we could prove the cops were lying. John also went over with me how little evidence the police actually had. Basically, their entire case was based on the ounce of crack they found in Will's car and the cell phone I let Will use while I was in the store. The only call on my phone connecting me to the drugs was the one Will made while I was in the store.

John Karafa and I had only one face-to-face meeting. Usually we communicated via mail and over the phone. He filed several motions asking that all charges against me be dropped for lack of evidence. The feds had charged me with possession with intent to distribute, but nothing in any of the police reports actually connected me to the dope in Will's car. Well, except for Will's statement that the dope was mine, not his. But that's not really proof, since it is his word against mine, and he was already known to be a drug dealer. John thought we had a good chance of getting the charges dropped, but the court denied every motion he filed leading up to my trial. Still, that didn't stop him from filing more.

A couple of days before my trial was scheduled to begin, I went to McDonald's to get something to eat. The guy behind the counter was a friend of mine named Corey. When he saw me, he asked, "Hey, man, you need a job?"

"No man," I said. "I'm fixing to go to jail."

"Nah man," Corey said as if he didn't believe me. "Just apply for the job. They really need people."

I don't know why but I said, "All right." I filled out an application and was hired on the spot to work the night shift. The next night I went to work and worked all night. When I got back to KPEP, I slept for a very short time and then got up, got dressed, and got in a car with my aunt and her boyfriend, who drove me to Grand Rapids for the start of my trial. Yes, I got a job the day before my trial started. I guess that means I hoped the truth was finally going to win out and I was going to go home a free man. I hoped it, but I didn't expect it.

During the ride to Grand Rapids, my aunt, her boyfriend, and I talked a lot, but the conversation was pretty depressing. My aunt cried through the entire drive. Over and over she and her boyfriend told me they could turn the car around and go back to Benton Harbor. Believe me, I wanted to say yes. I didn't want to go back to Grand Rapids because I had a really bad feeling about what was going to happen once I got there. Deep down I knew that if I walked into that federal courtroom, I was not going to go home for a very long time.

In America you are supposed to be innocent until proven guilty, but that's not how the system really works. You've got to prove beyond a reasonable doubt you didn't do something. If the court thinks you might have done something, you don't have a chance.

My lawyer met me in the lobby as soon as I walked into the courthouse. He started explaining what was supposed to happen. "This is the first day of the trial, and we're going to present evidence and see if this is going to go forward," I think he said. To be honest, my memory is a little clouded because I was in my own little world trying to figure everything out. I kept looking around wondering how I even ended up there. All I had done was ask a guy for a ride and let him use my cell phone while I went into a store to buy milk for my baby son. Why was I now in a federal courthouse? My lawyer explained a few more things, but nothing really registered. I felt as if I was in a nightmare that I couldn't wake up from.

When we first walked into the courtroom, the judge, the Honorable Robert Holmes Bell, looked at my lawyer and the prosecutor and said something like, "You don't have this figured out yet? You need to get this figured out."

I leaned over to John and asked what the judge was talking about. "Plea deal," he said. The next thing I knew, John and the prosecutor had left the courtroom. A few minutes later John returned and told me the prosecutor wanted to talk to me.

"About what?" I asked.

"They want to offer you a 5K1 agreement and give you downward departure in your time," John said.

This refers to section 5K1.1 of the Federal Sentencing Guidelines, and downward departure means a shorter sentence. At the time, most drug charges carried mandatory minimum sentences. But section 5K1.1 allows the court to reduce the sentence if the defendant gives substantial assistance to prosecutors that helps them arrest and convict bigger fish. Basically, the law says you get your sentence reduced if you rat out your friends or family or both.

"I don't care about that. I don't need no downward departure. I need to go home," I said.

"But this will let you go home sooner if you cooperate with them," John said.

"About what?" I said. "I ain't got nothing to do with any of this."

My lawyer looked a little frustrated. "So what do you want to do?" he asked.

I sat there for a minute, thinking. Finally I said, "If he's talking about sending me home, I'll talk to them."

"Good," John said.

John led me into an office and I sat across from the prosecutor. John took a seat next to me. The prosecutor just looked at me and said, "What do you have for me?"

"I ain't got nothing," I said. I wasn't being difficult. That was the truth.

The prosecutor didn't miss a beat. "Tell me about your cousins Ox and Wayne." Wayne is Ox's brother.

"I don't know anything about them," I said.

"They're your cousins, aren't they?" the prosecutor asked.

"Yeah. That don't mean nothing. I got a lot of cousins."

"I want them. Give me information about them and things will go easier for you today."

At this point I started to get really frustrated.

"I'm telling you," I said, "I don't know nothing about these two dudes. They're my cousins, which means I see them once in a while at my grandma's house. That's all I know, you know what I'm saying? When they leave my grandma's house, I have no knowledge of where they go and what they do. Period."

"I already have everything I need to go out and pick them up," the prosecutor shot back. He was starting to get hot.

"Then why are you messing with me?" I snapped. "If they're who you want, then go after them. You said you got all the information you need, so why are you asking me for more?"

I sat back in my chair and shook my head. This was ridiculous. The fact that the prosecutor asked me to give him information about my cousins that he could use to convict them told me he already knew I didn't have anything to do with any of this mess I was charged with. To me, it looked like the only reason they charged me with anything was to try to use me to get at my cousins.

"I ain't got nothing for you," I said.

The prosecutor turned red and started cussing at me. I stood up and said very loudly that I didn't need this, but in a little more colorful way. That set the prosecutor off even more.

John reached toward me and said, "Come on, Jameel, just chill. Just chill."

"No man," I said, "let's get out of this room. Let's get up and pull out of this conversation because it ain't going anywhere good." I headed toward the door with my lawyer right behind me.

Once we got out into the foyer, John pulled me over. "Jameel, what's going on, man? Why didn't you want to work with him?"

I could barely speak. "Man, this whole thing, it's garbage. He knows that ain't my dope. If he thought I had really done this, the trial would have just went right on. This whole thing, man, it's just BS. They want my cousin, so they're going hard after me, thinking that's the way to get to him."

The trial hadn't even started, but I knew how it was going to end. I didn't have a chance.

When we got back to the courtroom, Judge Bell pretty much laid into my attorney over two motions for dismissal John had filed on my behalf. He scolded

John for filing the motions later than he should have, talking to him like an annoyed teacher would to a little kid who was in trouble. The judge's tone and the way he spoke to my attorney told me right off that I was in trouble. When he finally let John present the motions, I knew Judge Bell was going to deny them. And he did. After that a jury was selected. Everyone on it was white and older than me.

My trial began a little before eleven in the morning. The whole thing started with Judge Bell making a speech to the jury about what to expect in the trial and how to make up their minds about the evidence in the case and whether or not they should believe a witness's testimony.

The prosecutor then got up and made his opening statement. I sat there trying to listen, but the whole time I kept asking myself how I got here. The prosecutor basically laid out his case and told the jury everything his witnesses were going to say.

When my lawyer got up to make his opening statement, the judge cut him off in the middle and told him not to make any arguments about my innocence. John apologized and then got back to his opening statement. Even before he finished the judge stopped him again and told John and the prosecutor to come up to the bench. I'm pretty sure I heard the judge tell my lawyer to shut up and not say anything else. I could be wrong, but when John was allowed to continue his opening statement, he cut it off with a short "I expect that by the close of the evidence in this case, the jury will find there is not sufficient evidence to prove beyond a reasonable doubt that defendant Jameel McGee possessed with intent to distribute cocaine base." Then he sat down. To me, the trial was already over. I knew I wasn't going home.

After the opening statements, the prosecution called its star witness, Officer Andrew Collins. I knew what he was going to say because of the police report, but I still couldn't believe how he lied so easily and how the jury ate it all up. The lies started with him talking about the phone call when his informant set up the drug buy. He said he recognized my voice and name from "contact prior to February 8, 2006."

I was like, *How? Man, you know you never laid eyes on me before that day.*

You didn't even know who I was. You thought I was Ox! I didn't dare say any
of this out loud, though.

My lawyer objected several times during Collins's testimony, but the judge
overruled every one.

When Collins got to the story of the arrest, nothing he said matched what
actually happened. He said he saw me in the car, which was a lie because I was
in the store when he got there. Then he said he drew his gun, which I never saw.
He also said he told me and Williams to put our hands up. I couldn't put my
hands up since I wasn't even in the car, but that wasn't the way Collins told it.
He said he saw me "lean over, make a furtive gesture toward the center console
of the vehicle, kind of turn with his shoulders into the center console, and then
turn back and put his hands up and look at the other officer." He repeated that
line a short time later and said he was positive I went toward the console, which
is where they found the rock of crack. Collins admitted they didn't find any
fingerprints on the bag of crack, but that didn't seem to bother anyone.

When my lawyer finally cross-examined Collins, John made a big deal out
of the fact that this was not my car and that there were no witnesses to what
had gone down at the arrest. Then he pressed Collins about my cell phone. I
thought this was going to help me. According to Collins's testimony, his informant allegedly called me several times to set up the buy, and he said that I had
called him. However, according to the original police report, the informant was
talking to Ox, not me. Collins danced around that one. He said he got the
names confused and stuck with that no matter how much John pressed him.

Then John went to the calls Collins said he overheard. As everyone with a
cell phone knows, all recent calls show up on a list on the phone. They looked
at the list of recent calls on my phone. There was only one call to the informant,
and that came at 2:31 when I was in the store and Williams used my phone. If
I had set up the buy, there would have been several calls in my call history starting around 11:00 in the morning. Collins explained that away by saying Nextel
phones show only the last call made, not all of them. I couldn't believe anyone
bought that load of crap, but apparently they did.

After John finished with Collins, the prosecutor got back up to ask more questions to make sure he didn't lose the case due to the fact that Collins originally thought he was talking to and looking for Ox, not me. Collins said he talked to so many potential drug dealers that day that he got confused over all the street names. He went on to say that he clarified it the next day by calling his confidential informant and confirming I was the guy with whom he had set up the buy.

My lawyer objected, saying there was a complete lack of foundation to his explanation and that the answer was hearsay since the informant wasn't there to answer that question himself. The judge overruled him.

After Collins, the prosecutor called Officer Lange to the stand, one of the two cops who had transported me to Grand Rapids. His testimony was as full of problems. He said that on the car ride from Benton Harbor to Grand Rapids I admitted to being in a house with Williams and my cousin Ox while they planned a drug deal with the informant. I don't know how Ox was supposed to be at my grandma's house and in Atlanta at the same time, but that wasn't a problem for Lange. According to him, I said I went to the store to buy groceries for my baby boy but then saw the bag of dope in the console when Will gave me a ride to the store. He said I admitted to picking it up and looking at it. I don't know how he came up with that, because I didn't even talk to those guys during the car ride, and I sure didn't pick up Will's bag of dope. I didn't even know he had it with him. Because Lange said all this, I now know, it was kind of a backup plan that could nail me as an accomplice to the dope deal, just in case the jury decided the crack in the car belonged to Will.

When the testimony was over and the judge gave his instructions to the jury, he told them they could find me guilty of the original charges or they could find me guilty of aiding and abetting Williams in his drug deal. Collins's testimony was all about the dealing charge while Lange's backed up the second charge. No one on the jury seemed to notice the two contradicted one another.

The prosecution rested. My lawyer didn't bring any witnesses for me. A lot of people had volunteered to testify about my character. Chris, my partner from the car wash, wanted to come, along with other people who knew me well. We told them all thanks, but I needed witnesses at the store, not character references. Unfortunately, no one was at the store the day I was arrested except Collins and Will and a few other uniformed officers. The cops weren't going to contradict Collins, and Will had already sold me out to save himself. The store security tape could have cleared me, but it was long gone.

Even without producing any witnesses, John thought we had a chance because the prosecution hadn't produced any evidence that connected me to the bag of dope. They didn't have any tape recordings of my voice setting up the drug deal. They didn't have any fingerprints on the bag of dope. They didn't have any video or photographs from the crime scene showing me in the car or making any kind of gestures toward the console. My lawyer asked the prosecution to produce each of these things, but they could not. The prosecution produced photos of the place where the drug deal went down, but they were all taken a few days before the trial.

There was even a lot of doubt about who Collins thought he was arresting that day, me or my cousin. All the prosecution had as evidence against me was my phone's one call to the confidential informant and the testimony of Andrew Collins. John thought that left room for reasonable doubt.

The jury didn't.

John prepared me for that. During one of the breaks, I could tell the whole thing was getting under his skin. Every one of his objections had been overruled, and the judge seemed annoyed that the trial was even happening. John looked at me and said, "It's rough, man. The way things are going, they're probably going to lock you up today."

"No man," I said, "that's crazy. We still have more days of this trial, don't we?"

"The judge wants to wrap it up quickly," he said. He let out a sigh. "I don't know," he said.

The judge had a last break before the closing arguments. I went over to talk to my aunt. "Well, I ain't leaving here today," I said and gave her everything in my pockets.

"What do you mean?" she said and started to cry. "You have to go to work tonight."

"My lawyer already told me it doesn't look good, and with all the stuff they're doing here . . . they ain't fixing to let me leave this place."

Before we went back in the courtroom, John came to me and said the prosecutor's 5K1 deal was still on the table. By this point I was ticked off and didn't have time for that BS. "I ain't got nothing to say to him," I said.

We went back into the courtroom for closing statements. John went first and made it clear the prosecution didn't have any real evidence against me. He said this was a case of mistaken identity and I had just been in the wrong place at the wrong time. The prosecutor then repeated what he had said in his opening statement.

After both finished, Judge Bell gave the jury long instructions on how they should make up their minds on this case. Basically, his instructions came down to one question: Do you believe Officer Collins or not? That's what this whole case came down to: Andrew Collins's claim that I had set up a drug deal and that he had caught me red handed.

The jury took no time at all to reach a verdict. They basically walked out, turned around and walked back in, and said, "Guilty as charged."

8

WAKE-UP CALL

Andrew

I was assigned to the narcotics unit on November 14, 2005, three months before I arrested Jameel. Three days after I arrested Jameel, I planted drugs in a case to make sure the suspects were strip-searched when they went to the county lockup. They were, and heroin was found hidden under the testicles of one of the guys I arrested.

That arrest made an impression on me. The main dealer I busted said to me, "Hey, Collins, I know you have a kid on the way. Tell you what, you leave me and my little brother and the rest of my family alone, and I'll pay you $1,200 a month. Cops don't make much. You need to take care of that baby."

I still find it very creepy that the guy knew so much about me. I turned down his offer. Two of the three people I busted in that stop went to federal prison. Two weeks later my little girl was born.

This dealer wasn't the only one who wanted me to leave him alone. By the summer of 2006, I started bragging to my friends that when drug dealers tried to get their kids to go to bed at night, they warned them, "You don't want Collins coming for you, do you?" A local radio station even talked about me and my antics on a daily basis. People used to call in to the show complaining about my tactics. I always laughed because I didn't do most of the things they accused me of doing, but I was glad they thought I did. To me, it confirmed that I was one tough cop who had crawled under the skin of the scum I was trying to get off the streets. It also confirmed my conviction that the city of Benton Harbor was lucky to have me on its side.

Complaints weren't just aired on the radio. People called in to the police department claiming I was too aggressive and abusive. Some charged me with being racist. I didn't feel I was, but my bosses thought I needed an older, more experienced partner who happened to be black. The way they saw it, he would keep me in line and help with public relations at the same time. When the department put B* and me together as partners, we already knew each other. He had interviewed me when I first applied to join the department. Back then he was a huge man, coming in at more than 400 pounds. Three years later he'd slimmed down to around 260. He was also very involved with the youth of Benton Harbor and had a good reputation in town. Our bosses hoped the goodwill many had for him might rub off on me.

B and I got along great from the start. I was a little worried, though, about how he might feel about some of my questionable tactics. I was also afraid my money skimming might come to an end. My fears were laid to rest not long after we started working together.

One afternoon I spotted a car about which I had received a tip earlier in the day. We followed the car in our unmarked vehicle until it stopped on the south side of town. Once the car stopped, I advised dispatch we were going to make contact with the two subjects inside. I claimed neither of them were wearing seat belts as my probable cause. B and I walked up to the driver who had already exited the vehicle. "Police officer," I said. "You need to get back in your vehicle. I have a few questions for you."

---

* To protect my former partner's privacy, I will not use his first or last name.

When the man spun around to get back in his car, he dropped what appeared to be a baggie of pot. That was my opening to search the vehicle. B and I also confirmed we both smelled the strong odor of burnt marijuana coming from the car. To top it off, the passenger was one of the usual suspects in town, the brother of one of the biggest dealers.

B and I removed both men from the vehicle and conducted a search. I arrested the driver for possession. I also searched the passenger and found what appeared to be marijuana shake in his pocket, that is, crumbs of marijuana. It could have been lint, but I called it pot. I did not, however, remove it and bag it as evidence. Instead, I let it fall to the ground.

When we searched the car, we found around $2,500 in the glove box, mostly in small denominations. All this went into our police report. What didn't go into the report was a portable PlayStation that went to B's house. I took it first, but when I realized I'd have to buy a charger for it, I lost interest. B took it off my hands.

When I found the money in the glove box, I realized I'd made a mistake by not keeping the shake. If we found marijuana in the car, we could seize the money under the civil forfeiture statute. I fixed that little problem when I wrote up the incident. I removed a baggie of dope from my stash and included it with the report. B went along with it. While typing up the report, I had an idea that I took to B. I told him, "If we say a snitch gave us information about this case, we can pay the snitch 10 percent of the money we seized. But since there is no snitch, we pocket that money. The two of us keep the $250 and split it down the middle." B didn't flinch. Now we were in this together.

B and I became very close over the next several months. We went after bigger and bigger fish, taking out some big-time drug dealers. Our methods were effective but not exactly legal. For example, I'd worked out a pretty good system to get any search warrant I wanted. On the form I falsely claimed to have met a confidential informant who gave me the name of a bigger dealer. I then supposedly gave the informant marked money to make a buy, followed him to the dealer's house, and watched him go inside. After he came out, I searched him and found drugs on him. The informant also told me he saw more drugs in the house. And guns. And cash. The lab tested the drugs and found them to be real. With all that information, the warrant was automatic, even though none of the story was true.

Every once in a while there actually was an informant who did everything I just explained, but most of the time I made it all up. The informant's name was real, but he had no idea I was using it. The drugs were also real, but I pulled them out of my Crown Royal bag that now had not only marijuana but also crack and heroin, whatever I needed to get a search warrant or more evidence to make an arrest stick. My partner and I split the money I supposedly paid my informant.

The whole system was a win-win as far as I was concerned. We got what we needed to conduct a search and bust a bad guy while also making a little profit for ourselves. As B and I made bigger and bigger busts, we seized even larger amounts of money. With time it became harder for us to keep our hands off the cash. The two of us were in this together, which gave us a sense of brotherhood, but I also found myself battling trust issues. Some days I wondered if B might turn me in. I also wondered if he might be taking money he wasn't sharing with me.

Throughout the process I found myself changing in other ways. Going all the way back to college I indulged in binge drinking even though I saw the destructive power of alcohol from how it had hurt my mom until she finally got sober. I don't know if it was what I saw on the streets as a cop or the crimes I committed myself or a combination of the two, but I started drinking more and more to numb myself. My marriage also started slipping. And there were days when I battled suicidal thoughts. At the same time I found myself becoming more and more calloused about the people and situations I encountered every day.

I didn't realize how far I had fallen until B and I responded to a reported shooting around ten o'clock one morning in mid-2007. In October 2004 I had attended a two-week course at a small college near Detroit and come away as a certified crime scene investigator. That's why I was called to the crime scene on this particular day. Someone had been shot and I needed to get over there to investigate the scene right away. Frankly, I was annoyed that my boss pulled me off narcotics for something like this. *The nerve of someone, getting shot on a day when I had so much planned for my real job.*

When I arrived on the scene, another officer led me around to the east side of the house where a kid who was maybe fifteen years old lay on his back with what appeared to be two bullet holes in his head. His body was maybe five feet away from a bedroom window that also had bullet holes in it. I looked at the boy's body and felt nothing. "So what's the story with this one?" I asked.

"Local gang member and marijuana dealer," another officer told me. "Apparently he went in to rob this house. The owner found out about it and was waiting for him. As soon as the kid got in the window, he popped him twice in the face."

"Looks like one less dirtbag for me to chase around," I joked. "Of course, it's too bad a dealer got killed. Guys like this are my job security." The other officer laughed along with me. The dead boy might as well have been a dead dog—that's how jaded I had become.

As a crime scene investigator, I was supposed to videotape the body and the entire exterior of the house so we could review the tape after the house was released back to the owner. No matter how hard we try, we usually miss some things initially and find them only when we go back and review the tape. Believe it or not, the perpetrator of a crime often hangs around the crime scene, and sometimes we find him on the tape, standing there and admiring his work.

On this day I got on with my job and made a very careful video catalog of everything. At one point I stood directly over the dead boy, zooming in on the bullet holes in his head, and an overwhelming sense of guilt came over me. I didn't feel bad for the boy. No, I felt guilty that I could not force myself to feel sorry for him no matter how hard I tried.

B was with me, and a short time later he let me know that a confidential informer had told him this house was owned by a big-time dealer. That meant there could be large amounts of drugs and money inside. B pulled me aside and said, "We need to get in that house before anyone else does." He didn't add, "so we can get the money," but he didn't need to. The look he gave me said it all. After all, this wasn't our first rodeo.

I quickly wrapped up my videotaping and switched from crime scene investigator to narcotics agent. I called the chief and told him B and I needed to get inside the house to search for drugs and evidence. I don't remember exactly what I said, but eventually I convinced him to let us do it. Before we could enter the house, I had to put together a search warrant. That wasn't a problem. I made up some facts and put them in a document, and we soon had our search warrant to look for evidence related to the shooting.

B and I were the first two officers in the house. A Berrien County Narcotics Division drug dog handler went with us. We started our search in the basement, where we found a large number of individually packaged bags of marijuana. After securing the evidence we headed upstairs. On the way out of the basement, B bumped his head against a stand-alone lamp. The bulb broke and cut his head. Blood went everywhere. I told him to get his head looked at, and I continued the search alone.

B ended up at the hospital, where he received a few stiches. I ended up in the upstairs master bedroom. From experience I knew this was the most likely place to find drugs or guns or money, since most dealers keep those things out of the places where their kids might find them. Even dealers have some common sense about parenting, I guess.

As I searched the master bedroom, I found two handguns, one of which turned out to be the weapon used to shoot the kid lying dead on the ground outside. Another officer joined me in the bedroom to help with the search. I thanked him and told him how much I appreciated his help, but inside I was cursing. He was looking for evidence; I was looking for cash. It didn't take long for me to find it. On the top shelf of the main closet I found a purse that contained around $1,500, mostly in small bills. The other officer watched as I opened the purse, which meant there was no way I could skim any for myself.

After securing the purse and cataloging the cash, I went back to searching the room. I went toward the dresser on the far side of the room while the other officer searched another closet. While his back was turned to me, I found a bulging sock in one of the dresser drawers. The bulge was a wad of cash with a rubber band around it. Casually, I slipped the wad into my pocket and continued my search.

I spent a few more hours at the house before everything was wrapped up and we could all head home. I briefed the chief on what I'd found, not mentioning the wad of bills I discovered in the sock. He commended me on a job well done. After all, we'd found pot packaged for distribution in the basement. It wasn't quite the haul I'd hoped to find, but along with the guns, it was a pretty good day.

About the time I finished my report, B was released from the hospital. I dropped by his house and his wife scolded me for not immediately calling her when B was hurt. I apologized with a laugh and a smile. "Come on," I told B, "I need you to help me finish up the report."

"Sorry, honey, I gotta go," he told his wife.

B and I both knew I didn't need any help with the report. The two of us needed to discuss what I'd found in the house. We always had this talk in our car. B was convinced the office we shared at the department was bugged. He even had suspicions about the squad car, which I thought was pretty funny. He didn't. He'd been a cop a lot longer than me and knew you could never be too careful.

We drove off in the general direction of the police station. I found an isolated spot and pulled over. "I found a little something I think you'll like." I pulled out the wad of cash, which I had already counted. There was $1,000 in all. I counted out $500 and handed it to him. "Here's your half," I said with a smile.

B was ecstatic. "Oh man, you are a good partner," he gushed.

"That's what partners do, bro. You're my guy. You'd do the same for me," I said and hoped it was true.

"I'm telling you, Collins, I am really touched by this. You cut me in when I wasn't even there. That . . . that means a lot to me."

B's reaction made me feel as if I had done a good and noble thing. After all, how many people would be so truthful and honest with their partner and cut them in on a large haul of cash when they didn't have to?

After we split the cash I drove B back to his house. Once I dropped him off I started toward my own home. Along the way it hit me what had really gone down that day. A fifteen-year-old boy had been gunned down, and all I cared about was the blood money I stole from the house of the man who shot him. An overwhelming sense of grief came over me. I pulled over and sat there for a long while, weeping over what I had become. This wasn't who I wanted to be when I dreamed of becoming a policeman. When I started with the department, I ended every day filled with joy and a sense of accomplishment. Back then I felt as though I was making a real, positive difference. Now I had become the very thing I hated.

I also worried about my marriage. My phone rang at all hours, day and night, mainly calls from B. He would call saying he'd just received a hot tip about a dealer, and out the door I'd run. Both our wives thought the two of us were covering affairs for one another. I didn't have a mistress, but I was still unfaithful to my wife with my job. It had become my all in all.

Sitting in my car, tears running down my face, I thought of all the ways I had let my wife down. I hated what I had done to her. I hated what I had done to B. I hated the thought of what might happen if I was found out. Deep down I knew I needed to make a change. I couldn't keep going like this.

But I did.

The next morning the shock over the dead fifteen-year-old had worn off. I got up, went to work, and kept right on doing exactly what I always did. By this point I believed I was in too deep to turn things around. I'd lied hundreds of times to my chief, to my captains, to judges, to juries, and to prosecutors in both state and federal cases. I realized I had also become financially dependent on the perks B and I created for ourselves. The pangs of conscience died down while I became even more aggressive both in trying to get drug dealers off the street and in profiting from them.

God fired one more warning shot across my bow that should have been enough. A few weeks before one of my arrests was scheduled to go to trial in a federal court, the US attorney on the case came to our department to go over the evidence and discuss our recollection of the incident. Everything sailed along fine until she said, "I need to talk to your informant myself. He may need to testify at the trial."

I tried to play it cool, but panic bells began to sound in my head. The informant listed had no idea he was associated with this case. He hadn't given us any information. I had simply used his name and a lot of false information to get a search warrant.

"That's not possible," I replied, hoping my voice didn't crack. "Standard procedure around here is to assure our CPIs [confidential paid informants] that they will never have to testify or go public. If one of them ever did, he'd be as good as dead, and we'd never get anyone else to talk to us again."

"Neither I nor the United States Attorney's Office cares what you promised him. I need your informant, and I need him by the end of the day today," she said. I could hear my heart beating in my ears. She must have heard it as well because she added, "And if you do not cooperate, Officer Collins, I will personally hunt him down and hand deliver him a subpoena to appear in federal court. Have I made myself clear?"

"Yes, very clear," I answered. "All right, well, if you'll excuse me, I need to contact my informant," I said as I got out of the room as quickly as possible. Before I got to my office, I had already hatched a plan. I decided to call a second informant who owed me big-time. A few months earlier I'd lied to the FBI about him and kept him from being indicted on federal charges. Instead, he did a couple of months in the county jail. Yep, this guy owed me, and now was the time to collect. I decided to tell the informant to claim to this nosy US attorney that he was the informant named on my search warrant. Before he met with her, I planned to tell him exactly what to say and how to say it, both to her and in court if he had to testify.

Before I could locate the guy's number, I realized that trusting a man like this to cover for me was both dangerous and stupid. I still called him, but instead of instructing him to come in and lie for me, I told him to find the person I had listed on the warrant and tell him to disappear for a few weeks because the FBI was after him. There is a legal term for what I did: *obstruction of justice*.

After making that call, I went back to the US attorney and told her I could not reach my informant but I had some people on the street looking for him. I don't know if she could see through my lies or not, but at this point my panic had given way to the adrenaline rush of living on the edge.

Once she left the office, I went into full-on cover-my-own-butt mode. B and I went to our captain and pushed him to make her back off. "You've been on the streets. You know what will happen if we lose our CPIs," we argued. He listened and went to bat for us. In the end, the US attorney backed off, but the experience scared me.

For the next few weeks I played it as straight as straight could be. I made sure the informants I listed on my search warrants had actually given me the information I claimed to have. But old habits die hard, and before I knew it, I was right back where I had been before. That's not entirely correct. I did not go back to where I was before. I went even further. The end, it seemed, was inevitable.

9

BECOMING WHAT THEY TOLD ME I WAS

Jameel

The moment my trial ended, my lawyer turned to me and said, "This is just jacked up. We have strong grounds for an appeal based on the chain of events that took place today. I'm going to file immediately."

"All right, all right. Cool," I said. If he hadn't given me that hope, I might have popped right then and there.

Either that day or the next, John filed a motion for a judgment of acquittal. Since Judge Bell was the judge who presided over my case, he was the one who made the decision on the motion. Exactly two weeks after he pronounced me guilty, he rejected the motion. He said we had not satisfied the burden of proof for the motion to be accepted. Once again I was guilty until I could prove myself innocent. The burden of proof was on me just like it had been since the moment Collins met me at the door of the store and whipped out his badge.

The day Judge Bell pronounced me guilty, I became the angriest man in the world. When word reached me that the motion had been denied, the anger boiling inside me hit another level. Then came the sentencing hearing, which took maybe five minutes. Once again, Judge Bell was in charge. He lectured me about what a horrible person I was. He said something like, "Your family members are all hardworking citizens, but not you. You chose to live like the scum on the street, taking the easy way out by dealing drugs. Why couldn't you be like them?"

My jaw dropped. He couldn't be talking to me. I'd worked my entire life, going back to when my twin brother and I worked in the blueberry fields when we were just kids. Work? Was he kidding me? My son's mother left me because she said I worked too many hours. Now this judge was lecturing me about how I chose the easy path? My life was anything but easy. My brother and I ended up in some of the worst foster-care families in the world because my home life was so bad growing up. There were days we ran away and slept on the streets to get away from the beatings we endured. I never had the easy way, and I *certainly* never turned to drugs. Most of the misery I lived through as a little kid came from my parents' addictions. I hated drugs. And I loved to work.

Listening to the judge's lecture, I felt like a volcano about to explode. This judge was talking down to me, saying all this stuff about me when he had no idea who I was. To him, I was just another drug dealer. I was pretty sure he was mad at me because I had the nerve to claim I was innocent and force this whole thing to go to trial. To him, I should have cut a deal because I was guilty before the jury was even seated. He didn't care that I had nothing to do with any of this. The prosecutor didn't care. The jury didn't care. And Collins, well, he sure didn't care. He knew the truth. He knew I had nothing to do with the crack he found in Will's car, but he came after me anyway and made up this whole story that put me right here, standing before some judge who had the nerve to lecture me about hard work when all I had ever done was work hard my entire life.

"And for that," Judge Bell continued, "you will receive the maximum sentence for your crime: ten years to be served in a federal prison."

Ten years! *Ten years!* For what? I hadn't done anything wrong.

John was standing next to me and could see I was about to explode. He put his hands on my shoulders and whispered, "Man, just be cool. You don't want to make this worse. Be cool."

Behind me, my family members who had come up for the hearing started crying. I turned to them and a calm came over me. "It's okay," I said to them. "At least I don't have life. I'll be home eventually. It's all right."

Judge Bell did give me a chance to make a final statement. I guess this was where I was supposed to express my regret for the mess I'd made of my life and the trouble I'd caused the world. Instead, I said, "I didn't know you could get in so much trouble for letting someone use your cell phone." With that, the officers in charge came over and took me away.

I went straight from the courtroom to a holding cell, where I sat for a couple of hours. Finally, some federal marshals came in, shackled me, and led me to a van that drove me to the federal prison processing center in Milan, Michigan. The drive took a couple of hours. As soon as they unloaded me in Milan, I was strip-searched, then placed in a dorm-type cell with around twenty other guys. The dorm had four sets of bunk beds, which meant the room was supposed to hold eight guys, not twenty. Every person in the room was there on drug-related charges.

From the moment I stepped out of the courtroom and into the holding cell, I made up my mind I didn't want nothing to do with nobody. I planned to just keep to myself and do the time. I didn't know if I could make it ten years. My mind got really dark. For the first time ever, I thought about ending my own life. I had no real hope and no reason to trust that the future was going to be any better than the past. The way I saw it, I might as well give up and check out. What was the point of going on? Eventually I got over these suicidal thoughts, but I still gave up on life. Based on everything I'd seen and experienced, life had already given up on me.

The dorm cell was crowded, but I found a spot to put my things and sat down. Everyone in the room was talking about their case, and all of them were angry about getting caught. I didn't say anything. I sure didn't speak up and tell how I'd been railroaded by some cop and given ten years for something I didn't do. No one wanted to hear that, and getting all high and mighty about being innocent wasn't going to do me any good in here. Instead, I just kept my mouth shut and listened, which was not good for my state of mind.

A lot of the guys had been busted with kilos of drugs. Kilos, not grams, like I had been accused of. That wasn't a big deal to me. That was their situation, not mine. But then I heard them talk about their sentences. These guys were looking at less time than me. A lot less. I sat there boiling inside, wondering how I got ten years for twenty-eight grams I didn't even have and these guys got four or five years for kilos they admitted were theirs? That told me how jacked up the whole system really is. Dark thoughts came back to me. I hoped that when I laid down and went to sleep I wouldn't wake up.

I remained in the processing center for a few weeks. I can't remember exactly how long because everything sort of runs together now. Like I said, my mind wasn't in a good place then. I bounced back and forth between anger and depression. The only thing that kept me going was the hope that my appeal would go through and I'd get out of this place. Since an appellate court, not Judge Bell, would make the decision on my appeal, I thought maybe I had a chance.

One day while still in the processing center, I went down to the television room and took a seat at a table to watch some TV. There was a Koran on the table, which didn't mean much to me and didn't bother me. I have some Muslim family members, so I knew a few things about Islam. I am a Christian, but I figured live and let live. If someone wanted to read the Koran, that was cool. That didn't have anything to do with me. Then a guy came over and sat down next to me. I didn't want to get into any deep conversations, so I sort of acknowledged he was there and went back to watching TV. The guy pointed to the Koran and told me he was Muslim.

"Okay, cool," I said.

He then started in on the differences between the Bible and the Koran. I tried to downplay it and said something like, "Yeah, I got some family that's

Muslim, but I'm Christian, so, yeah, you know, cool." I really wanted to just watch television, but this guy wanted to take the conversation deeper. He started to get really worked up, like he was trying to convince me that Islam was the only way.

Finally, I said to him, "You know, man, I don't really want to hear any more of this, all right? I'm cool with whatever you believe, you know. Now, if it's okay with you, I just want to watch some television."

The guy made it very clear very fast that it wasn't okay with him. He stood up and started telling me what he planned to do to me. "I'm going to beat your face in," he yelled at me.

He should have just left me alone. I'm not a big guy, but I know how to take care of myself. Growing up in Benton Harbor and spending as much time on the streets as I did, you had to know how to fight to survive. And I knew how to fight. My brother and I boxed when we were kids, as in actually getting into a boxing ring with gloves and protective headgear and the whole thing.

I leaned back and looked at this guy and was like, "Whoa. Really? You want to fight me?"

"That's right," the guy said in a way that showed he meant business.

The other guys in the room saw what was going down and started making room. A few of them were people I knew from Benton Harbor.

"Wow. Okay," I said. "You want to do it right here?" At this point I didn't care about anything. I didn't get all loud and up in his face, but inside . . . in-side, man, I was out of control.

The guy looked around the television room and said something about not fighting there because we'd get caught. There was an open room right next door, so I invited him to follow me in there. He did.

The first time I hit the guy, it was to defend myself. The punch put him on the ground. But I didn't stop with one punch. I fell on top of him and started swinging. I wasn't hitting an inmate who started an argument with me in the television room. Every time I threw a punch, I was hitting Officer Andrew Collins who had put me here. And I was hitting Officer Lange, the other cop who testified against me. And I was hitting Judge Bell and the jury and everyone else who had put me in this prison. But mostly I was hitting Andrew Collins over and over again.

Next thing I knew, my homeboys from Benton Harbor were dragging me off the guy and out of the room. If they hadn't, I'm afraid I might have killed him. I didn't want to kill him. I didn't want to hurt him. But I did want to kill Andrew Collins.

For the next three years I thought about little else. And I knew how I wanted to do it. I didn't plan on using a gun or a knife. Those are too quick and easy. No, I planned on beating Collins to death, punching him over and over and over again until I couldn't lift my arms. I am not nor have I ever really been a violent man. I had never wanted to hurt or kill anyone until this point. The longer I was in prison, though, the more I wanted to exact my revenge one punch at a time on the man who put me there.

To my great surprise, I did not get into trouble over the fight. I expected to face some kind of disciplinary action, but none came. The day after the fight, I went and found the guy I'd beaten up so I could apologize to him. I walked into his cell and said, "Hey, what's up, man?"

"Yeah man, what's up?" he replied. Then before I could say a word, he said, "I want to say I'm sorry."

"Nah man, that's why I came down here to find ya," I said. "I shouldn't have taken it as far as I did. I had a lot of stuff done to me, which is why I ended up in here. I took all my frustration out on you. I'm sorry. I ain't that type of guy. Man, if you'd just left me alone, we'd been cool, but when you didn't, I took everything I was feeling inside out on you."

"I'm sorry, man," he said, "and I want you to know I don't have no beef with you. I'm not gonna be trying to come back and sneak up on you, none of that. I'm gonna be straight up front with you from now on."

"All right. I ain't worried about it. You just be you around me and we'll be fine. Hopefully we can get past this," I said.

A couple of days later the guards came and told me to gather my things because I was being transferred. The Milan processing center is directly across from a federal prison. Not everyone who goes through the processing center ends up at the Milan prison—a lot of them are sent to other places around the country. Me, I just had to pick up my stuff and walk through some gates to the prison next door. Of course they strip-searched me when I arrived, even though I was coming from a federal holding center.

The guy with whom I'd gotten into the fight was transferred at the same time. He ended up in a cell a couple of doors down from me. I learned his last name was Hernandez. I never knew his first name. We never got into another fight. The two of us started talking and became pretty good friends. He was one of the few guys I talked to in prison. Hernandez was a good artist, so a few months later I went to him with a request. Since I'd boxed growing up, I decided I'd like boxing gloves tattooed on my arm. He did it for me. Over the next few years the two of us got tight.

While I was in Milan, I also met a cousin I didn't know I had. I'd seen this guy around the prison and he seemed okay. One day I heard him mention one of my cousins as his cousin. When I heard that I was like, "Whoa, what are you talking about? That's my cousin." The two of us started talking and found out we were related. (I have a really big family.) After that we looked out for each other.

My only other real friend in Milan was a guy named James, but everyone called him Jimmy. It turned out his case was exactly like mine, except he admitted to me he was guilty. He was mad, but mad that he'd been caught. Not only was he arrested with the exact same amount of crack I'd been charged with, but by coincidence he had the same name as the confidential informer Collins had used against me. The only difference between him and the informant was one had dark skin and one had light. When I heard his name, I was like, *Oh my gosh, that can't be true.* But it was.

Jimmy and I hit it off from the start. We'd met at the processing center and both ended up in Milan. The two of us spent a lot of time together. With everyone else I kept my mouth shut and let people know to keep their distance. I didn't have anything against anyone; I just wanted to be left alone. Jimmy was one of the few guys I let get close. He asked me many times why I never said anything to anybody. I told him, "That's just the way it is, man. I don't want to know anything about them, and I don't want them to know anything about me. I just want to be left alone."

That wasn't as easy as it sounds.

One day my cousin and I were watching TV in the television room, minding our own business. Another guy walked in and came straight over to me. "That's my spot," he said.

I looked around. The entire room was empty except for my cousin and me. I sort of shook my head and said, "Just pick another chair."

He didn't move. "That's my chair and I'm not sitting anywhere else."

I gave my cousin a look. "Listen, man, nobody has assigned seats around here. I suggest you sit somewhere else 'cause I ain't moving," I said.

"Get out of my chair," he demanded.

I looked to one side, then back at him. I felt anger rising up inside me. This guy didn't make me angry; I was always angry from being in there. Most days I was able to keep it pushed down inside me, but it didn't take much to pull it out. This guy pushing me wasn't much, but it was enough.

"I really think you better leave me alone, because this ain't cool," I said.

He walked toward the television, paused for a moment, then came back. "You better get out of my spot or I'm going to make you pay," he said.

"Whoa. Wait a minute. You're going to do what to who?"

He repeated his threat and added, "You think this is a game? This ain't no game." Then he walked to the door and looked both directions to make sure no officers were nearby.

"You really want to fight me over a spot? Okay. Let's go out in the hallway and get this over with." I got up and walked out. My cell was a short way down the hall, so I walked there to put away my headphones (you had to use headphones to hear the television). I also stacked all the things I'd need to take with me to the hole so I'd be ready when they sent me there for fighting.

"What are you waiting on?!" the guy yelled at me. He'd followed me to my cell.

"Man, you really have no idea," I said. I walked out of my cell and went down to the end of the hallway. The guy came running and took a big swing at me. That's the only one he got to throw. I threw one punch in self-defense and didn't stop hitting him until, once again, my friends dragged me off of him. The moment he started pushing me in the television room, he ceased to be another inmate. Andrew Collins had come into the prison and I took him out.

The fight scared me but not because I thought I might get hurt. I didn't care about that. What scared me was how I didn't care about anything. The most dangerous people in prison are those who have nothing to lose. They don't care if they live or die, which means they will probably end up killing someone or getting themselves killed or both. I never, ever thought I could become one of those guys, but slowly I was becoming one.

I had several other fights in between the two I've described. Every time I got a little better at taking my guy out, and every time I pushed it closer to the edge. It was only a matter of time before something really bad happened. I had become somebody I never knew, somebody I did not want to be. I knew I needed to change, but I didn't know how. To change meant letting go of the anger that consumed me, to let go of my chance of getting even with the cop who had destroyed my life.

I didn't want to do that.

I wanted him to feel the pain I lived with every day. I wanted him to get his, and I wanted to be the guy to give it to him. But if I stayed on the path I was on, I would never get the chance because I'd be dead long before the federal government let me back out on the streets.

10

BUSTED

Andrew

I woke up excited on Tuesday, February 19, 2008. The week before, an informant had told me that a guy we called Pistol Pete had a house full of crack and guns. Because I was a narcotics detective, I was off the day before for Presidents' Day. I went into work anyway to put together a search warrant, and now I was going to serve it. Like I often did, I falsified most of the information in the warrant, even though I didn't need to. If I'd been more patient and put in a little more time and work, I could have produced a clean search warrant. But I never even thought about doing that. A cop like me didn't have to play by the rules. That's what I told myself. The truth was I was too lazy and sloppy to do the hard work the job called for. Not that I cared. I had a search warrant for a big-time drug dealer, and today I was going to make a huge bust.

I needed this bust for a lot of reasons. The week before, I had gone on trial myself on an assault charge. Back in November 2007 I'd been in a bar fight and ended up fracturing a bouncer's skull. Even though I was arrested and charged and went on trial, I never missed a day of work. The department told me to keep them informed about the case as it progressed, and that was it. The trial had ended, but the judge hadn't handed down his verdict. Busting Pistol Pete, a major drug dealer, might put me back in the good graces of the department and myself.

Most days I didn't have to be at the office until ten, but on February 19 I arrived early. Like I said, this was going to be a big day. But the search didn't turn out quite like I had hoped. B and I and a team of cops searched Pistol Pete's house, but it was clean. No dope. No guns. Nothing. I drove back to the station feeling frustrated and more than a little on edge.

My captain greeted me at the door. He called B and me into his office and told us to have a seat. "Collins, we have a problem," he started. "I'm going to be straight with you. Your work has become sloppy to the point of being a disgrace to police work. I thought the suspension you had a few months ago might wake you up [I had been suspended for five days when I was caught falsifying information on a search warrant], but apparently it didn't. You're going to be demoted back to road patrol."

I sat there stunned and hurt, but the hurt didn't last long. Instead, a sense of relief came over me. My wife and I had already talked about the possibility of me leaving the narcotics unit because of the pressure that came with the job. But I had ruled that out because of the perks that came with being on the narcotics unit, like a take-home car, a free cell phone, a flexible schedule—to say nothing of the bonuses B and I regularly created for ourselves. I wasn't sure how we could make it on just a cop's salary. Now that I didn't have a choice, I thought we could figure it out. I'd dug a deep hole for myself as a narcotics officer, and this appeared to be my way out.

For a few moments I didn't say anything. I just stared at the floor, thinking. Finally, I looked up and said, "Okay, Captain. I'm sorry I let you down. Thanks for letting me stay in the department."

"I know you have some things on tap today," he said. "Wrap everything up this morning, then turn your keys over to your partner. After that you can go home and have your uniforms cleaned and pressed to get ready for road patrol tomorrow."

My mind immediately went to what I was going to tell my wife. Choosing to step away from the narcotics team was one thing. How was I going to tell her I had been demoted? I couldn't tell her my captain said I'd become a disgrace to police work. I was lost in thought when I heard the captain say, "We'll need to search your office and your vehicle first."

Cue the dramatic music.

My heart stuck in my throat. All the air was sucked out of the room. I could not breathe because I knew what they might find. Somehow I pulled it together enough to say, "Okay. I have nothing to hide." Unfortunately, my voice cracked on the last word. I don't know if my captain heard it, but I was positive he knew I was lying.

B and I followed the captain down the stairs to the office the two of us shared. I opened the door and followed them inside. The captain immediately went to my desk and started opening drawers. The whole time my eyes were glued on the small lockbox I kept under my desk. From my vantage point I could just see the corner of it, but the captain couldn't see it from where he stood. If he looked under the desk, I knew I was as good as gone. Thankfully he didn't, at least not then. He went through every drawer but found nothing of interest. There were a couple of marijuana blunts in the top drawer that he either didn't see or chose to ignore. When he got up and moved to B's desk, I started to breathe again.

The captain went through B's desk rather quickly. He spotted a small lockbox underneath and asked B to open it, which he did. After finding nothing of note in the box, the captain went into the small locker room area of our office. Small is an understatement. The room was partitioned off by a wooden door. Inside were two lockers where B and I kept our personal and work-related items. A file cabinet sat off to one side and contained all the files on our confidential informants. My duty bag lay on the floor of the room. I hadn't used it in a very long time, at least from the time B and I started using this office. Back in the day I carried around all the tools I needed to do my job: latex gloves, supplies, even my paperwork. Frankly I'd forgotten about it.

When the captain started to open it, I wasn't worried. I looked toward B and he mouthed, "I didn't do this. It's not my fault." I gave him a little shrug of the shoulders as if to say, "No problem," and looked away. Once the captain left my desk, I'd stopped worrying. I'd always felt more than a little bulletproof as a cop. That arrogance began to return.

My confidence evaporated when the captain looked up at me from the duty bag and said, "What's this?" In his hand he held a plastic baggie with smaller bags of packaged marijuana. He also pulled out a small digital scale. Dealers use scales like it to weigh out drugs for sale. "You have any kind of explanation for these, Collins?"

I started to say, "I was wondering where that was," but I thought better of it. I muttered something—I can't remember what—but I had no explanation. To be honest, I was as shocked as he was that he found those things in my bag. The scale I could explain. Several officers carried them to get an accurate weight of the drugs they confiscated in arrests. But the pot—I knew that didn't look good.

"I'll have to contact the prosecutor's office about this and report it to him. You may well face charges of possession with intent to deliver," he said.

In that moment the captain ceased to be *my* captain, a man who had tried to mentor and mold me. Instead, it was clear he cared only about being the man who cleaned up the Benton Harbor Police Department and rooted out dirty cops. And I instantly saw him as the embodiment of evil, the man who threatened my freedom and livelihood.

The captain then moved to my locker and went straight for a small cashew can on the top shelf. Popping off the lid, he looked into the can, then back at me. He held the can out toward me. "What's this?" he asked.

From his perspective it had to look like trail mix for a pill popper. The can contained all sorts of prescription medicines, pills of all shapes and sizes and colors. A few months earlier I had confiscated it from a car full of outsiders who had clearly come to Benton Harbor in search of narcotics. When I first opened the can, I nearly fell over laughing. I could hardly believe these people had crammed so many different pills into a peanut can. I kept the can as a souvenir. None of the pills were narcotics, so I didn't see keeping it as a big deal. Every time I told the story about the car full of pill heads, I pulled out the can and showed it to my friends. Everyone always got a good laugh out of it. I didn't dare try to tell this to the captain. I doubted he'd see much humor in it.

Before walking out of the locker room, the captain found a locked bag that held B's riot gear. "Whose is this?" he asked.

"Yeah, uh, mine," B said.

"You have the key?"

"Not on me."

"Then we'll have to take it upstairs to the fire department and have them cut the lock off," the captain said.

By this time I could not look him in the eye. I stood off to one side, my eyes glued to the floor. As bad as the inspection had been, I knew it could have been a lot worse. I thought I might still be able to explain the pot and the scale and even the can of pills. Best-case scenario was I would be suspended for a month, maybe more. That I could handle. More likely I would get fired. I didn't think they would prosecute me for what he'd found so far. Now I just wanted to get him out of my office and have this whole thing over and done with.

The captain stepped toward the door, but then, for reasons I will never know, he turned back toward my desk. He stood over it for a few moments, then bent down and looked underneath. My whole body went numb. I watched in slow motion as he reached under my desk and pulled out the lockbox. "What's in here, Collins?" he asked.

"Yeah, I've got no idea," I lied. "It was in here when we moved into this office. I just shoved it under my desk and pretty much forgot about it." I knew he didn't buy a word of it.

"Either of you have a key to it?" he asked.

B and I both shook our heads no.

"Looks like we'll have to have the fire department cut this open too," he said. He then handed me the box to carry. "My office. Let's go," he said as he led the way out the door. B fell in behind him, his duty bag in his hand. I paused for a moment at the door to lock it and to buy some time to figure out a way to get rid of this box that held my Crown Royal bag filled with drugs. The moment the captain got a look at what was inside, life as I knew it was over. Period.

For a split second I contemplated running out the back door of the police station and returning with an empty box. *And how guilty will that make you look?* I thought. Instead, I started down the hallway, following the captain and B, falling a little farther behind them. As we approached a bathroom, I took the lockbox key out of my coat pocket, dashed into the bathroom, threw open the lockbox, and tossed the Crown Royal bag into the garbage can. I knew I needed to bury it deep under the other trash, but I didn't have time. As quickly as I could, I caught up with the captain and B. The captain turned around, looked me in the eye, and asked, "Why are you suddenly acting like a criminal?"

I gave him my best "What are you talking about?" look and then pulled a digital recorder out of my pocket. "My partner dropped this. I stopped to pick it up for him," I lied. B took the recorder without saying a word. The captain just looked at me, then turned and continued toward his office.

The moment we stepped into the captain's office he asked for the lockbox. "And your keys," he said. I handed him both, knowing this was the end. He thumbed through my keys and found the one to the lockbox. Anger flashed in his eyes as he looked at me before opening the box. When he discovered the box was empty, he nearly lost it. He spun around to his phone and called the prosecutor's office. Everything became a blur, but I could hear him talking about filing charges against me for the pot he found in my duty bag. He then called the K-9 officer and told him to bring the drug dog to the station. "Start in Collins's office and see if you can find the trail from his office to mine," he said. When he hung up the phone, he asked me, "Do you have drugs hidden on your body?"

For the first time in a long time, I told the truth. "No sir."

He didn't press the point. The conversation then turned to who would escort the K-9 officer and drug dog around the station.

While his back was turned to me, I said to B, "Man, this is garbage." At the same time I motioned with my hands to let him know I had dropped the drugs in the trash.

The captain's door opened, and a detective entered to ask the captain a question. The look on his face told me he had no clue what was going on. This was my chance. Many times I'd looked the other way when this detective went over the top in his aggressive tactics during an arrest. More than once I saw him slam a suspect down on the hood of a patrol car and maul him while yelling, "Stop resisting! Stop resisting!" I'd even covered for him when someone charged him with using excessive force. He had to cover for me now. That's what cops do. We called it the thin blue line, where cops stick together even when they know the other is in the wrong.

After the detective asked his question and before he could leave, I said, "Captain, I really have to go. Do you mind if he escorts me to the restroom?" Suspects were never allowed to go anywhere by themselves, and I was now a suspect, not a cop.

"Yeah. Go," he said as he motioned me out the door. Looking at the detective, he ordered, "Keep an eye on him. Make sure he doesn't get rid of anything."

The detective led me to a different restroom than the one in which I'd tossed the bag. As soon as the bathroom door closed behind us, I started spilling my guts. "I tossed a purple bag in the trash can in the other restroom. If the captain finds it, I'm finished. I need you to get it out of here. I'll explain everything later, I promise, but for now, I need you to do this for me. My life is in your hands," I pleaded.

"What's in the bag?" he asked.

I dropped my head. My whole body began to shake. Finally, I looked up, broken. "Dope, man. There's dope in the bag. I need you to get rid of it for me. Captain will crucify me if he catches me with it. I promise, it's not what it looks like. I'll explain everything later. Please, please, do this for me."

"Yeah, Collins, man, don't worry about it," he said. "I got you covered." The look on his face did nothing to reassure me he meant what he said. We went back to the captain's office, where I found they had opened B's bag. There was nothing bad inside. I sat down and tried to relax, but I felt as if I was about to throw up. I looked over at B. For a black man, he sure looked pale. No matter how hard I tried, I could not get him to make eye contact with me. He sat stock still, studying his shoes.

Eventually I pulled out my phone and called the detective. I tried to make it sound as though I were talking to my wife. "Have you taken care of that bill?" I asked. "It has to be done today." The whole time the captain sat only two feet away from me. The detective on the other end of the phone kept telling me to stand by.

I hung up.

The captain's phone rang. "What did you find?" Long pause. "Okay." He hung up and looked at me and B. "You two, step outside."

Apparently the drug dog officer was on his way. As he came down the hallway, I quickly called out to him, "What did you find?"

"I found the bag," he replied.

"What was inside?"

"Marijuana."

I let out a sigh of relief. I thought the other detective must have destroyed the other drugs that had been in it. "Anything else?" I asked, hopeful.

"Crack and heroin," he said.

I could not say a word. Game over.

Later I learned the detective I had trusted in the bathroom went straight to his supervisor, not the other bathroom, and told him everything I'd said. The two of them then went to the bathroom, found the bag, and started processing the room as a crime scene.

The captain came up to me. "You probably don't want to say anything else until you speak with a lawyer." That was the reading of my Miranda rights. Then he asked for my gun and badge and instructed me to go with him to the chief's office.

My meeting with the chief didn't take long. The captain told him what they'd found, and the chief simply replied, "Prosecute him."

The dam broke. The chief had always been one of my biggest supporters. Not now. Not ever again. I wept openly and began to blubber something about how I had always been a good cop.

"Keep quiet," I was told. They called in the sergeant on duty and instructed him to walk me out of the station and drive me home. "You are suspended with pay until further notice," they told me.

I knew that was only a formality. I was now on the other side of the line. I was just one more person caught with drugs in Benton Harbor. I knew what the future held, and it wasn't going to be good.

11

LET IT GO

Jameel

The only place I found peace in the Federal Correctional Institution in Milan came through the job I had there. All my life, music has been my passion. When I had planned on going to college, back before my first arrest when I was fifteen, I wanted to major in something related to music. Working in a studio had always been my dream job. After my mom pleaded guilty for me and sent me off to prison the first time, the closest I ever got to that dream was installing car stereos for my friends. But when I got to Milan, I found it had an organized music program complete with a recording studio and all kinds of instruments: keyboard, piano, guitar, bass, drum, you name it. When I saw that, I was like, *Cool. This is the place for me.*

I ended up getting a job as the quartermaster of the studio. That meant I was in charge of all the music. I worked with guys as they came in and played and recorded music. On days when no one came in to record, I would listen to music for hours. I found great peace in that. Outside of the music room, though, peace was hard to find.

I got in a couple more fights after the one that scared

me. Both started in the television room. Most prison fights start in the television room, the basketball court, or the weight pile in the yard. The first fight began when a guy I recognized from the weight pile started making loud comments in the television room about anyone from Benton Harbor. This guy was serious about his weights. He could bench-press around five hundred pounds. I lifted most days, but I topped out around two hundred fifty. This guy was like the weight pile champ and he knew it.

Maybe that's why he came after me with his Benton Harbor comments. He couldn't have been after anyone else because the first time he spoke up, there were just a few of us in the room, and I was the only one from Benton Harbor. I ignored him because I didn't want to get into another fight.

Later that day he did it again, this time when the room was packed with people. He pointed at me and called me out. I gave it right back to him and made some comments about people from Detroit, which was where he was from. He didn't like what I said, but he was asking for it. Other people in the room looked at me as though I were crazy for going back after someone so ripped, but I knew being able to bench five hundred pounds didn't mean a thing in a fight.

Everything should have ended in the television room. He'd insulted me. I'd insulted him. We were even. Again, I wasn't looking for a fight, so I decided to call it a night and went back to my cell. I was about to lie down when I heard, "What's up, ———?" he said, using a degrading word. He'd followed me from the television room to my cell.

I turned around and saw him standing in my cell door. "What's your problem, man?" I asked.

"That stuff you said in there," he said. "That's my problem."

"Listen, man," I said, "you had your little piece to say and I said my piece. That makes us even. I ain't trying to fight you. I don't have time for that. I'm fixing to go to sleep."

"Oh, you're about to go to sleep one way or another," he said.

"Serious, man? You really want to fight?" I was annoyed.

"You don't want this," he said, puffing out his chest.

"No, I don't," I said, "so I'm going to go lay down." I turned to get in my bunk when he pushed me from the side. I turned around and pushed him back. He then came at me like he was going to grab me. He didn't get close enough to lay a hand on me. I punched him twice in the mouth and dropped him. That's when the rage came back. I fell on him and just started punching. At one point I grabbed a chair and started hitting him in the head.

The next thing I knew, I felt someone touching me from behind and saying, "Jameel, Jameel, come on, man." Eventually the gentle touch from behind became arms wrapping around me, pulling me backward. "Come on, Jameel. You don't want to do this. Stop." I dropped the chair. "Don't do nothing, bro. I'm just holding you so you can cool down." That's when I realized Hernandez, my Muslim friend with whom I'd had the fight at the processing center, was pulling me back.

The guy on the ground looked bad. Blood poured out of deep cuts over both of his eyes. His friends came and took him back to his cell. One of the guys stitched up the gashes. The next few days the guy wore a skull cap low to cover them to keep the guards from seeing he'd been in a fight. If you were caught fighting, you'd go to the hole, even if you got the worst of it.

The next day I went to see the guy I'd beat up to apologize for going so far. Just like the other guys, he apologized first.

"It's cool," I said. "I ain't got no issue with you."

A few days later I was back in the television room and a really tall white guy came in and started griping about the channel I was watching. He wanted to change the channel to his show, but the rule of the television room is that whoever is there first chooses the channel until his show is over. This tall guy either didn't know the rule or didn't care, because he kept pressing and pressing and wouldn't let it go until I finally pushed him out of my way. The guy was really shocked that someone so much smaller would push him back. He charged at me and I dropped him. When I turned around, I saw a lot of people staring through the big window that looked into the hallway. I was like, "Ah,

man," and went immediately to my cell to get my things together for a trip to
the hole.

Sure enough, the guards put us on lockdown and had everyone take off
their shirts and put their hands through the cell bars so they could see who had
been fighting. They started at the end of the cellblock farthest from me, but I
knew it was just a matter of time before they came for me. Off in the distance
I heard them open a cell and pull someone out. It was the tall white guy I had
dropped. I waited. Then I heard another cell open. They pulled out the guy
who could bench five hundred pounds and carted him off. And that was it.

The guards had two guys—one black, one white—and as far as they were
concerned, they had everyone they needed. All that night I waited for the
guards to come and get me. I figured it was just a matter of time before one or
both of these guys spilled their guts. But the guards never came. They should
have, though, because I was a bomb primed to go off.

My attorney had written me to tell me all my appeals had been denied. He
was sorry, but there was nothing else he could do. There was one last ditch appeal he planned to make, but the odds of its working were next to impossible.
In all likelihood, this prison cell was going to be my home for a long time. The
rage boiling inside me grew to a whole new level. That's what pushed me to
keep beating the one guy with a chair. Just like before, I wasn't beating him; I
was beating Andrew Collins, the cop who had put me here. If Hernandez
hadn't grabbed me, I hate to think how far I might have gone. It was just a matter of time before I went too far. Every fight was just a dress rehearsal for what
I planned to do to Collins when I saw him.

I planned on killing him.

Not long after the two guys I beat up went to the hole for fighting, I noticed
something in my room I'd never noticed before. Lying on a table was a dusty
Gideon's Bible. Apparently the Bible had been lying on the table since the day
I moved in, but I had never touched it. On this day, however, it was like the
Bible was calling to me. I had to pick it up. I had to start reading.

I opened it to the first book, Genesis, and started reading. After five verses I heard a voice speak to my spirit saying, *Let it go.* The voice might as well have been talking out loud, because it was that clear. *Let it go* ran through my mind over and over. *Let it go.* This was a long time before the movie *Frozen,* so I wasn't hearing the words to that song. But the words did sound like a song that started playing in my head. *Let it go.*

I stopped reading, but I could not put down that Bible. *Let it go.* I didn't leave my cell for a very long time. I sat there on my bunk, holding the Bible, hearing the same words over and over in my head. *Let it go.*

After a while my head started to pound. My mind turned to all the Bible verses I'd read or heard when I was younger. Romans 12:19 in particular jumped out at me: "Dearly beloved, avenge not yourselves, but rather give place unto wrath: for it is written, Vengeance is mine; I will repay, saith the Lord" (KJV). I also kept hearing the words of 2 Chronicles 20:15: "For the battle is not yours, but God's" (KJV). I wasn't even sure where 2 Chronicles was in the Bible, but I knew it was in there somewhere. I'd heard sermons on it before. Now the words kept running through my head, along with the same chorus, *Let it go.* God was telling me to leave revenge to him.

I had not touched a Bible or even thought about anything linked to God since I was arrested on February 8, 2006. When I got to the prison in Milan, I didn't go running back to God like I had when my mom had pleaded guilty for me when I was a juvenile or when I went back on a parole violation. I didn't run to God when Collins arrested me because I knew the police didn't have any hard evidence against me. And as angry as I was, I had held out hope that the appeals court would see what Judge Bell and my jury did not. I didn't think I needed divine intervention for people to see what I thought should have been obvious to everyone. Every time one of my appeals was denied, I became too angry to think about God. But now God had come looking for me.

All these thoughts ran around in my head until I thought it might split open. *What does this all mean?* I asked myself. *Is God telling me I need to let go of all I'm dealing with, because I can't do that. I have to handle it.* I *have to take care of this situation. If I get back home and don't do something about Collins, then everyone is going to look at me like I'm crazy.* To me, not getting revenge for what Collins did to me was the same as telling everyone, "Yeah, I did it. I'm guilty." I couldn't do that.

The battle is not yours, but God's, I heard in my spirit.

No, no, no! I gotta fight this. I gotta take care of this fight.

"Vengeance is mine; I will repay, saith the Lord."

I stood up and put the Bible back on the table. If I stayed in my cell another minute I was going to lose my mind. I had to think. I went outside to the track that runs around the perimeter of the prison yard. Some guys run on the track, but most people just walk. That's what I did. I walked laps as *Let it go* echoed in my head.

For the next several hours I walked around and around and around that track. I didn't talk to anyone and no one bothered me. Because I never talked to anyone, no one thought it odd to see me keeping to myself. I didn't talk to God, either. Instead, I walked and thought about my life. I reflected on my whole life, from the time I was a little kid until the present.

Since the day I first went to prison at age fifteen, I'd always blamed others for what had happened to me. My mom had pleaded guilty for me to the carjacking charges, even though I was with my dad when the crime happened. Walking around the track, I took another look at how I'd ended up in that situation. My dad had warned me not to go for a ride with my friends, but I told him nothing bad would happen. I realized I had simply taken the easy way out. I should have listened to him. That was on me. It didn't matter what happened after that. I could have chosen to listen to my father and stayed home. If I had, my life might have turned out very different.

The same was true of the ride I took to the store with Will. I went back to that day as I walked around the track. When I asked someone to give me a ride to the store, I did it because I was in a hurry. But Will wasn't. By the time he was finally ready to go, I could have walked to the store and back. *Why didn't*

I? I asked myself. *Why didn't I?* Sure it was cold, but when you live in Michigan, you get used to the cold. And why did I accept a ride from somebody I didn't know? I didn't even know his real name until after I'd been arrested. Hadn't I learned my lesson from what happened when I was fifteen? I should have been smarter than that. I should have just walked, but instead, I took the easy way out. That was also on me. If I had just walked to the store rather than waiting around for a ride with someone I didn't know, I would not be in prison now.

I'd spent so much time being angry at everyone who put me here that I failed to recognize I could have avoided the whole situation by not putting myself in a position where something bad could happen to me. That didn't excuse the lies told against me in my trial, but it did make me realize I had to stop blaming everyone else and spending all my time being consumed by anger and a desire for revenge. All anger had done so far was turn me into someone I didn't like, someone I did not want to be.

I had to let it all go. That was the hardest thing for me, which made me start praying.

More guys had come out on the yard, but no one paid much attention to me as I continued walking laps around the track. And God and I had a long talk. I did not pour out all my complaints to him over what had been done to me. I prayed about my situation, but not in a "God, you need to do something to these people" kind of way. Instead, I told him how everything I had been doing wasn't working. If I stayed on this path, I was going to end up in prison for a very long time, not because of the original drug charges, but because I was becoming a menace to both the prison and myself. I had not yet been busted for fighting, but I knew it was only a matter of time before I hurt someone so bad that I might even kill him. And the worst part was I had nothing against anybody inside these walls. All my anger was directed at the people who put me here, especially Andrew Collins.

Let it go.

I thought about my son, who was now four years old but didn't know me at all. *I want to get to know my son,* I told God. *I want to raise him or at least be in his life. If I keep doing what I'm doing, that's not going to happen. The last thing I want is for my son to only know me as a man in prison. I came here an innocent man, but I'm not anymore. I didn't do the things they accused me of doing, but I'm in a bad place now. God, I need to change.*

I kept walking, but now I stopped talking and started listening to God. He'd already been talking long before I got outside. I listened to what he had said to me with the Bible verses and with the three little words that kept running through my head: *Let it go.* Finally, I chose to do just that. I let it go. I gave my anger and my desire for revenge over to him. All of it.

The moment I turned loose of my anger, God planted inside me a desire to open up to others. That was something completely new for me. From the day they had led me out of Judge Bell's courtroom, I closed myself off from everyone except a couple of people. I didn't want to get to know anybody, and I didn't want them to know me, because I did not deserve to be here. Now I understood it didn't matter that I didn't deserve to be here. I *was* here, and shutting everyone out wasn't making this place any easier for me. Minding my own business and telling everyone else to keep out had contributed to a lot of the fights I'd had. I did not come across as an innocent man upset over the injustices of the system. I came across as rude and angry, someone just looking for a fight. God showed me that had to change.

Eventually I stopped walking and started back to my cell for the night. I prayed again before I went to bed. *God,* I prayed, *when I wake up tomorrow, I want to feel like I am at home. I want to feel different, better.* Then I went to sleep.

When I woke up the next morning, my anger was gone. Instead, I felt this overwhelming desire to talk to somebody I did not know, somebody I had shut out and kept from talking to me in the past. As soon as I walked out of my cell, I saw an older gentleman who'd tried to talk to me off and on the entire time I'd been in the Milan prison. Every day he asked me how I was doing, and I always just pushed him back. Today I went over to him.

"Hey, how are you doing today?"

The man looked from side to side, then looked at me as if wondering what in the world had just happened. "What? You can talk?" he said with a smile.

"Yeah man. I can talk." I laughed.

"So what's your name?" he asked.

"Jameel. I'm from Benton Harbor." I then talked awhile longer, telling him more about me.

"Man, what has been your deal all these months? What did you do?" he said.

"Honestly, I didn't do nothing," I said.

He sort of shook his head. "Usually when people come in here and act like you been acting, they've committed murders or something really bad like that," he said.

I laughed. "Nah man, ain't nothing like that."

"Well, when you get the time, we can, you know, sit down and talk about it now that I know you ain't all on edge."

"Cool," I said, "we can do that." As I walked away I glanced back and noticed him talking to another guy. The older gentleman made a motion with his hand to indicate he thought I was crazy. I couldn't blame him. I just laughed and went on my way.

This conversation was at least a start. I knew I had to keep making an effort to connect with people every day. I started playing cards and lifting weights with the other guys, just talking and getting to know them. Since this prison was going to be my home for the next six or seven years, I needed to treat it that way. I was tired of being alone.

A few days after my breakthrough on the walking track, a letter came for me. This was no ordinary letter. I had to sign for it, which meant it was some kind of official document. I'd had a really good week in the band room, helping guys record some music, and I was feeling pretty good. The envelope made me nervous. Inside was a letter from John, my attorney. The news wasn't good. The appeals court had denied John's final, last-ditch appeal to get me out. I sat on the edge of my bed for several minutes, holding the letter, thinking about what it meant. *That's it then,* I thought. *There is absolutely nothing else I can do about any of this. It is what it is—ten years, federal prison.*

Every other denied appeal had left me boiling inside. This letter was my test. Had I really let it go? Had I truly surrendered my situation to God? Then I remembered the verse from 2 Chronicles: "The battle is not yours, but God's." I thought to myself, *This isn't my fight. God's got it. Jameel, just let it go.*

And I did.

12

"SO YOU'RE GUILTY, THEN?"

Andrew

After the sergeant drove me home from the station, I told my wife I was in trouble for some drugs I hadn't handled correctly. "I should have put them into evidence, but I never did and now they want to prosecute me over it," I said. I'd lived a lie for so long I actually believed what I told her. When the story broke on the news that night and my face was plastered across the screen, I believe doubts crept into my wife's mind about me.

Even though the situation could not have looked worse, I still thought I could find a way out of it. Surely if I explained that in my zeal to get more drugs off the street I had simply forgotten to log these drugs into evidence, my superiors would understand that. I'd admit I'd been lazy and sloppy. I rehearsed what I planned to say over and over in my head until I nearly believed it myself.

My plan for redemption blew up when I met with the police union attorney. The first words out of his mouth were, "I'm not sure what you did, but this is getting big."

I tried to play it cool. I gave him that old "I don't know what you're talking about" look and said, "Big? Really? How?"

"Now the FBI is involved. They're already talking about indicting you for a racketeering conspiracy. Investigators are interviewing all your confidential informants because apparently the police suspect you lied about your controlled buys. Word is the money that was supposed to go to the CPIs went into your pocket," he said.

I tried not to react, but I knew I was dead where I stood. Only one other person on earth knew about my pocketing money. B must have come clean. But if he had, he would have had to tell on himself as well. Or he may have simply lied to save himself. The thin blue line had failed me again.

I could hardly force words out of my mouth. Finally, I managed to spit out, "So what can I do?"

"If you resign immediately, they might back off since they will have given the public what they want, which is to get rid of you," he said.

"Okay," I said. My little plan to save my job was no longer an option. Now I hoped to avoid going to prison. With great reservation on my part, the union attorney and I went to the chief's office, where I signed my resignation papers. I could not believe my dream was dying like this. On the way out of the station, I ran into the captain and B. The two were walking along, joking with one another, until they saw me. B's eyes dropped to the floor. The captain stared a hole through me. I recognized the look. It was the same one I gave suspects after I'd nailed them.

When I returned home I collapsed onto a chair in the living room and felt the weight of all my failures crashing down on me. Back in my bedroom I had a .357 Magnum hidden where my daughter could not accidentally find it. Sitting alone in my living room, alternating between crying jags and fits of anger, I thought how easy it would be to grab my gun and go out into the woods behind our house and end it all. With any luck, my wife wouldn't be the one to find me. Maybe no one would. Everyone could then get on with their lives. They'd all be better off without me.

Thankfully, my wife came home from work before I put my plan into action. She took one look at me and said, "I think you should go talk to Pastor Brian." Brian Rumor was the pastor at New Life Baptist Church in St. Joseph. I'd been there a few times with my wife and daughter. The church seemed loving, and Pastor Brian genuinely seemed to care about people. But he also had a way of talking in his sermons about whatever I had done wrong the week before. I didn't know who had been talking to him about me, but he seemed to know all my secret sins. That's why I didn't attend very often. I hated coming out of Sunday services feeling so bad about myself.

When I went to see him on February 20, 2008, I knew I couldn't feel any worse about myself or life than I already did. If he'd watched the news or read a newspaper, he probably had a pretty good idea of what I wanted to talk about when I made the appointment. I might not have gone except Pastor Brian had been a cop before he became a pastor. If anyone could understand the pressures I'd felt and why I did what I did, it was him.

Pastor Brian welcomed me into his office and offered me a seat. After a long, awkward silence, he asked, "What's going on?" His tone of voice struck me. He didn't sound like a cop conducting an investigation. To me he sounded like a compassionate friend comforting someone who had just lost a family member.

"Can I trust you with a secret?" I asked.

Pastor Brian rocked back in his chair and took a deep breath. "Anything you tell me will be held in the strictest confidence. If the president of the United States subpoenaed me to his office and asked me about you, I could not tell him anything you tell me."

I let out a long sigh. "Okay." Another delay. "Well, I guess I should start from the beginning." I then dumped everything on him in what felt like one breath.

When I finally finished talking, Pastor Brian looked across at me and said, "Boy, you are in a mess of trouble."

That wasn't what I expected to hear. I wanted him to make me feel better, to give me hope that everything was going to turn out all right. Instead, he told me what I already knew. Doubt overwhelmed me. I wondered why I had made the horrible mistake of saying anything to him. What a terrible counselor! My every instinct was to get up and run out. I might have, but I could not muster up the energy to even stand, much less run.

Pastor Brian let me hang there for a few moments before adding, "How's your relationship with Jesus?"

Jesus? What does this have to do with Jesus? I'm not sure why I was so surprised that a Baptist preacher wanted to talk to me about Jesus, but it was as if I had run into a brick wall with that question. I rattled off stories of how my grandfather had been a youth pastor and how my grandmother had been a pillar of the church.

"That's all well and good, but I didn't ask about your family. I asked about you. How's *your* relationship with Jesus?" he asked again. Memories flooded back of going to church as a boy when I was seven or eight and praying a prayer asking Jesus to save me.

Finally, I confessed, "I don't deserve Jesus! Didn't you hear me tell you what I've done? I don't deserve him."

"None of us do," he said with an intent look. "We're all sinners, fallen short of God's glory. None of us 'deserve' Jesus. That's the beauty of grace. Andrew, I believe you when you say you accepted Jesus into your life as your Savior as a boy, but you've never trusted him to be the Lord of your life, to guide your steps, to help you see how to live."

My mind flashed back to all the events that had led me to this place. I'd been in charge of my life and I'd made a mess of it. Looking ahead, I couldn't see anything, at least not anything good. When death looks to be your best option, you've probably hit bottom.

"I'm at the end of myself and I need someone else to take over because I've screwed everything up royally," I said.

"All right then," he said. "Why don't you kneel down here on the floor with me."

I agreed, but it put me a little on edge. I'd prayed many times in my life, but I never felt compelled to get down on my knees. Before I could say anything, Pastor Brian started talking to God about me as though he were talking to his own dad. I'd never heard anyone pray like that. He told God all I had done as if God hadn't been in the room when I'd spilled my guts. The funny thing is, the more Pastor Brian talked to God, the more I was right there with him, agreeing and talking to God myself. The Father was in the room and I could feel his presence. Before I got up off my knees, I confessed to my Father all I had done and asked him to save me based on what Jesus did for me when he died on the cross. I also asked him to fill my heart and take over my life. I turned everything over to him, even though there wasn't much to give.

The more I prayed and the more I confessed, the more I felt him lift the burden off my shoulders. I didn't feel better about myself. I experienced something better. By the time I got up off my knees, I didn't matter anymore. My life was now his and his life was now mine. I had a new start and a new life. I felt free, and tears of joy flowed. And the whole mess with the police department and the FBI investigation and a possible indictment? It all disappeared, and my wife and daughter and I lived happily ever after. The end.

Except, we didn't.

We started going to church together as a family, and I continued talking to Pastor Brian. People within the church recognized me, which I expected given the news coverage, but I never felt judged. My life was changing for the better, but I still faced a mess of my own making.

When I resigned from the police department, I received a check for unused vacation time as well as payment for the money I had paid into my retirement. Three months after leaving the department, though, our money was nearly gone. Thankfully, I found a temporary summer job driving for UPS. If everything went well, I would have a good chance of being hired on permanently.

But my wife and I weren't doing quite so well. Even before everything blew up with my old job, the two of us were having problems. After she learned I'd been living a lie for most of our married life, the strain got even worse. We hardly talked. I felt like a failure because I couldn't support the family financially. Given all I'd put my wife through, I thought she probably also had trouble trusting me. I couldn't blame her.

And then there was the stress of not knowing what was going to happen once the FBI finished its investigation. I read my Bible like I never had before, and I prayed with an intensity I didn't know was possible, but the elephant never left the room. We couldn't make plans for the future because we had no idea if I even had a future.

The strain hit its peak one day when I was home alone with my little girl. I looked outside and saw a familiar SUV pull quickly into my driveway. I recognized the vehicle right away as one that belonged to an FBI agent named Al with whom I'd worked closely on several drug cases. Now he was at my house. He had to be here to arrest me.

The moment the SUV came to a stop, I grabbed my two-year-old daughter and ran into a closet, closing the door behind us. She thought the whole thing was a game and started to laugh, but I held my finger up to my lips to tell her to be quiet while also trying to act like I was playing along. A loud knock rang out from the door. I held my breath. A vision of Al dragging me out of the closet in handcuffs while my little girl screamed and cried ran through my head. I reached down to my pocket for my phone only to realize I'd left it in the living room. Now I had no way of calling someone to come get her.

Another knock, even louder this time. Then another. Finally, I heard a car door close. Slowly I opened the closet door and did an army crawl across the floor to the window. Out in the driveway I saw two women get back in the vehicle. They'd left *Watchtower* magazines from the Jehovah's Witnesses at my door.

August rolled around. Six months had passed since I had resigned. My wife and I went to a wedding in a quiet little town on the shores of Lake Michigan while our daughter stayed with her grandparents. Getting away from Benton Harbor, just the two of us, worked wonders for our relationship. The two of us walked hand in hand through little shops and on the shore. It almost felt as though we were the ones getting married. By the time we came home, everything had changed between us.

I tried to call in sick to UPS the day after we returned. It was raining and windy and seemed like the perfect day to cuddle up with my wife in bed and escape the worries of the world. My boss, however, didn't see it that way. He already had two or three other drivers out. I had to go in. I got up, dressed, and reported to work.

Six hours later I was writhing in pain, my UPS truck resting against the garage of a house. My brakes had failed on the slick streets, sending me through an intersection. I hit the front passenger-side corner panel of a pickup truck, which caused it to do a complete 180 in the intersection. Time slowed. I remember thinking, *That wasn't so bad.* Then I saw the tree. My truck bounced off the tree and didn't stop moving until I hit the garage.

My left leg was pinned between the seat and what was left of the dashboard. Somehow I managed to pull it free myself. I hobbled over to check on the driver of the pickup truck. As it turned out, my leg was broken and so were my spirits. Because of the accident I knew my chances of landing a permanent driver's job were nil.

I didn't know how I could face my wife after this. We'd just had what felt like a fresh start. Now I feared we were back to square one. *At least things can't get any worse,* I thought.

Two days later my phone rang. On the other end was a friend from the police department. Turns out not everyone on the department had abandoned me after all. "We need to meet tonight," he said.

"I don't know," I replied. "I just had an accident, and I don't know if my wife will understand if I take off all of a sudden for a meeting."

"This is pretty serious, Andrew," he said in a way that let me know I had to see him.

"Let me put Krissy on the phone and have you explain things to her," I said.

I gave my wife the phone. She went into our bedroom to talk while I sat on the living room floor and played with our daughter. A few minutes later she came back. The look on her face told me something was wrong.

"What did he say?" I asked.

"He said he needed to talk to you tonight because some things are going down with the criminal investigation," she said. "I asked him if you were going to jail and he said, 'Not tonight.'"

"Then I better go see him," I said.

"Yeah."

The news was bad. "A grand jury has been called for your case. At least two officers on the department have been subpoenaed to testify against you," my friend said. He paused for a moment. "It looks really bad because, you know . . ."

He didn't have to say the rest. I knew what was coming.

When I returned home I went straight to my daughter's room and sat on the floor to watch her sleep. I was afraid to talk to my wife because I didn't want to face reality. With all that had already happened in 2008, I couldn't add a separation or divorce to the mix. I thought if I didn't say the words, they weren't true.

Part of me was angry with God. *I've come clean with him. Why doesn't he fix all this?* Those thoughts didn't last long. God hadn't done this. I did it to myself. That's why I sat in the dark in my daughter's room. I wanted to be a dad, watching over and protecting my daughter.

Oh, God, how could I have done this to her?

As I sat in the dark, hugging my knees to my chest, I saw my wife standing in the bedroom door. After what felt like an eternity, she asked, "What did he say?"

I couldn't talk. My tongue was stuck to the roof of my mouth.

"What's going on?" I could tell she was getting annoyed.

I didn't say a word until she simply said, "Seriously?"

I looked up at her. A look of disappointment and anger flashed from her eyes. I looked away, trying to work up the courage to say the words. Finally, I simply said, "I'm getting indicted."

Krissy turned and walked away without saying a word. Fear paralyzed me as the realization hit that I was going to prison. I sat on the floor of my daughter's room in the dark and wept over the thought of my little girl growing up without me.

When I knew a federal indictment was inevitable, I immediately started looking for a good defense lawyer with extensive experience in the federal justice system. I didn't just need a defense attorney who could fight for me. I needed one who knew the ins and outs of the federal system, which is different from Michigan's state system.

A friend referred me to Frank Stanley in Grand Rapids. The first time we met he explained how everything we talked about was protected under attorney-client privilege. Then he added, "If you're guilty, the best thing to do is minimize the damage. If you're innocent, I'll fight for you with everything I have. Now, I must tell you, the federal government does not like to lose cases they prosecute, especially in a case involving police corruption. I guarantee you they're going to come at you with all they've got as well."

"I understand," I said. Then I sat there for several moments, searching for the right place to begin my story. Other than Pastor Brian, I had not told anyone everything I had done, not even my wife. Overcome with shame, I couldn't look Frank in the eye. Instead, I sat there staring at the floor, trying to force my mouth to form words.

"So you're guilty, then?" Frank simply said.

Still staring at the floor, I nodded my head. That simple acknowledgment freed me to begin to speak. "Yes," I said softly. Then the words began to flow, and I told him my entire story in great detail. Once I finished, I asked, "Would you be willing to represent me?"

"Yes, of course," Frank said. That settled it. I had found my attorney, my advocate. After discussing possible next steps, we shook hands and I drove home. Before I even arrived at home, he called to tell me he'd arranged a meeting for me with the lead prosecutor on my case.

A few days later I was back in Frank's office. That's when I first heard the extent of the government's case against me. "They're ready to indict on at least six felony counts, including obstruction of justice, racketeering, possession of crack with intent to deliver, possession of marijuana with intent to distribute, possession of heroin with intent to distribute, and civil rights charges."

I swallowed hard in shock. "So what does all of that mean?"

"If you are convicted on all six counts, the mandatory minimum sentence is somewhere around twenty years." I ran the numbers in my head in relation to my daughter's age. That's when it hit me: I stood a good chance of missing all of her grade school, junior high, and high school years, as well as college.

The mandatory minimum sentence . . . When I was a cop I used those words like a hammer to break suspects and get them to rat out their partners in crime. Now that I was on this side of the equation, everything looked different.

"So what can we do?" I asked, desperate.

"The prosecutor is a real black-and-white kind of guy. He told me if you are willing to work with him and cooperate with the investigation, they might be willing to work with us on the level of charges," Frank said.

"Anything," I said. "I'll do whatever I have to do."

Frank went on to explain that the US Attorney's office had offered me a proffer agreement. This was not a plea agreement where I would do *X* and get *Y.* Instead, the prosecutors said they were willing to consider filing a 5K1 motion if I cooperated with their investigation. The motion gave the judge discretion to sentence me as he saw fit. The great part of a proffer agreement is that if at some point during the process I gave incriminating information about myself that the prosecutors didn't already have, they could not use that information against me. "But since they've pretty much thrown every charge in the book at you already, I don't think that's going to be a problem," Frank joked.

I felt relieved by the proffer agreement. If it went through, I might be reunited with my daughter before she graduated from college after all. Even more important to me was the prospect of regaining some shred of integrity that I had thrown away over the previous few years. Telling the whole truth without shading my stories to shift blame to others felt like a good first step.

My sense of relief was short lived. Frank went on to tell me that none other than the Honorable Judge Bell had my case. The mention of his name made me sick to the pit of my stomach. Judge Bell had a well-earned reputation for being hard nosed. I'd testified in his court against men he'd put away in prison for a long time. On many of those occasions, I had lied. When Judge Bell put those facts together, I didn't expect much mercy from him.

"Judge Bell? He can't hear my case. I've testified in front of him too many times. That's a conflict of interest!" I pleaded with Frank.

"Well, maybe," he said, "but there's nothing we can do about it."

I had no choice but to trust his judgment.

My first proffer meeting came in early September at the FBI office in St. Joseph. I knew the office well. I'd been there many times as a cop. Rather than meet with one of the prosecutors, I was scheduled to sit down with FBI agents, and not just any agents. The lead detective, an agent named Al, was in charge of this interview. To say I was nervous was an understatement. Over the years I had become very familiar with his work. As a cop I appreciated how he made bad guys crumble. Now I wished I was meeting anyone but him.

We took our seats and made some pleasant small talk. Al treated me like we were still old friends, until he asked his first question, which I thought was a joke: "Do you have any offshore bank accounts?"

I gave a small chuckle, and then I saw the look on Al's face. He was dead serious. The government obviously believed I'd run some sort of organization generating enough cash that it needed to be hidden away in a Swiss bank. "No," I answered truthfully. "All the money I skimmed was spent long, long ago."

"I need to explain the rules of these meetings to you, Mr. Collins," Al said. "You must be completely truthful. If we catch you in one lie, everything you've told us will be thrown out. Do you understand this?"

"Yes sir."

"Then why don't we start from the beginning," he said.

"Okay. When I was eight years old, I stole a package of Life Savers from the store down the block from my house." I meant this as a joke, as a way of lightening the mood. No one thought it was funny.

"Let's stay more specific to your wrongdoings as a member of the Benton Harbor Police Department," Al replied in a serious tone. He was in no mood for levity.

I let out a sigh and said, "All right." I then told him how my partner, B, and I operated within the narcotics division. I started off with the story of the arrest where we took the video-game system and skimmed off money for ourselves by using the name of a fake informant.

Al stopped me. "I find it very hard to believe your partner was involved in your activity," he said.

"You told me I had to tell the whole truth, and this is the whole truth. I started doing things before we became partners, but once we were put together, the two of us did these things together."

Al had a surprised look. "Your former partner has been a crucial part of the task force assembled to investigate you," he said.

I felt as though I'd been punched in the gut. Had B sold me out? Had he told them everything, except how we were partners in every sense of the word? I hoped that wasn't the case.

"I don't know about that, but I can tell you what the two of us did on a regular basis." I went on to describe in detail how we falsified search warrants off little or no information and how I used the drugs stashed in my office to justify them. I explained that if I stated in a warrant that I'd made a controlled buy of crack, I took the crack out of my stash and pocketed the money. "That's what I did with the drugs found in my office. Once or twice we planted some on suspects, but that was rare."

"So you didn't sell the drugs yourself?" Al asked.

His question surprised me. "Excuse me?" I asked.

"You did not take drugs from dealers and then turn around and sell them yourself?" he clarified.

"No! No way. I never did anything like that."

"That's a relief," Al said with a slight smile.

At the end of our first meeting, Al shook my hand and made a promise. "In light of all you've said, I'm going to work as hard to keep you out of prison as I've been working to put you behind bars these past six months," he vowed.

I thanked him, but I kept thinking about that last line. This mess I'd made for myself was much deeper than I had ever imagined.

Over the next three months I had multiple meetings with Al. I passed the polygraph, during which they asked me about B's involvement. Later, Al had me wear a wire and talk to B myself to try to get him on tape admitting to the things we did together so the FBI could go after him. I felt very uncomfortable doing this, and B did not trap himself.

In the meeting after I passed the polygraph test, I walked in and discovered a stack of file folders on the table. "The county prosecutor's office has a huge pile of complaints against you," Al said. "They started rolling in as soon as the news broke the day you were caught. These are some of the files for cases on which you worked. Some, not all. We'll get to them all eventually. For now you can help us clear up this mess by going through these with us one at a time and letting us know which cases were compromised."

I guess I had known this was coming, but I dreaded it. Thanks to my greed and lies, the very people I worked so hard to get off the streets were now going to go free. If I'd done my police work the way I knew I was supposed to, without cutting corners, these convictions would have all stood.

FBI agents and I then went through the case files, one at a time. When I found ones in which I'd lied to obtain a search warrant or faked an informant or changed the police reports or lied to get a conviction, Al sent them to the prosecutor's office. The charges against these defendants were then dropped or, if the defendants were already in prison, their convictions were overturned and they went free. Over the next few months, which is how long it took me to go through all the files, nearly sixty cases were dropped or convictions overturned.

The Sunday night after Thanksgiving my phone rang. It was Al. He wanted me to come in the next day to take another polygraph test. I explained to him it was my daughter's birthday and we had plans to take her to Chuck E. Cheese's to celebrate. He assured me it wouldn't take long, so I agreed to meet him the next morning.

After I hung up the phone, I sat there for a long time, thinking. Krissy came over and asked what was going on. When I told her, she said something about how odd this seemed. Over the previous three months of meetings, Al had settled into a fairly regular routine. This didn't fit it.

The moment I walked into the FBI office the next morning I knew I was in trouble. There were no files stacked on the conference room table. The polygraph machine was not in its usual place, and the agent who administered the test was nowhere to be seen. There was only Al standing at one end of the room, waiting for me. As soon as he saw me, he said, "The indictment came down. You're under arrest."

"But my daughter's birthday . . ." I blurted out.

"The indictment came down last week, but I didn't want to arrest you before Thanksgiving," he said. I didn't believe him.

Two other agents appeared and handcuffed me. I was led to a waiting car and we left for Grand Rapids, where I was to be booked. Thankfully the two agents allowed me to make a couple of phone calls during the hour-long drive. I first called my wife and told her what had happened. We cried together, less over my arrest, which we both knew was coming, but over the timing of it.

After I hung up I wondered how many more birthdays I was going to miss.

13

FREE AT LAST

Jameel

Two, maybe three days after my final appeal was denied, I received another letter informing me the federal prison system had decided to move me to Level I custody. The lower the level, the less risk you pose to the prison system. The letter offered me the chance to transfer from Milan, which was a Level IV prison, to the trustee camp that didn't even have a real fence in Terre Haute, Indiana. I didn't have to give the decision a moment's thought. I was ready to get out of Milan. The place didn't exactly hold a lot of fond memories for me.

There are actually two federal prisons in Terre Haute. The camp was the smaller of the two, with a limited number of inmates. Right across the street sits the United States Penitentiary (USP), which is one bad place. Its level is off the charts. The Oklahoma City bomber, Timothy McVeigh, was housed and executed there.

When I arrived in Terre Haute, I went through the usual routine: strip-searched and all of that. Then I was placed in a cell for the night. The next morning I awoke to bells clanging like an escape alarm had gone off. I had no idea what was going on. The guards came in and escorted me and another thirteen or so guys across the street to USP.

Oh, God! What's happening? I prayed with every step. I don't think I've ever prayed as hard as I did when they led us through the gates of USP. When we got inside, they didn't strip-search us. Instead, the officers took us straight to the kitchen. On the way I keep looking around. I felt as if I were looking straight into hell. *Oh man, I hope they aren't fixing to keep me in here.*

Once they had us in the kitchen, one of the officers told us what was going on. "The entire prison is on lockdown right now. Until that changes, you gentlemen will work the kitchen," he said.

I don't remember if he told us or if I heard it from one of the other trustees, but apparently there'd been a stabbing. I was told in no uncertain terms to watch myself because this was a dangerous place. I never thought it possible to miss Milan, but I did that day. *What have I gotten myself into?* I wondered.

The first group came in for breakfast. These guys had a look about them I didn't see very often in Milan. To be honest, they probably had the same look I carried until God finally got me to let it go. Guards were everywhere, more than normal, but looking around, I realized if something went down, there wasn't anything the guards could do about it. I didn't have a beef with anyone here, but that didn't make me safe. Desperate people who feel they have nothing to lose will sometimes go after people who do. I went back into survival mode, hardly speaking to anyone, keeping mainly to myself.

After we had worked in the kitchen all day, the officers escorted my group back across the street to the camp. I'd never been so glad to see a prison facility in my life. The next morning, though, we were back in USP, and the next day and the next. They had us spend one night in USP, which I did not particularly enjoy. Security there was unlike anything I'd ever seen. Even the bathrooms were locked down.

The days I spent working in the kitchen passed pretty easily until one afternoon. I was dishing out food behind the counter when I heard a noise in the dining area. An inmate suddenly took off running across the tabletops. He jumped one and then another, moving toward a guy who was sitting at a table, eating and minding his own business. The next thing I knew, the guy running across the tables stabbed the other dude in the neck. The guy never even knew what happened to him until it was too late. I looked over at one of the other trustees, and we both had a terrified look on our faces. Both of us knew that could have been us with the shiv in our necks. That night I prayed a lot. Even though I had gone into survival mode, I wasn't about to go into it alone.

Thankfully, the day after the stabbing in the USP dining room, they took us off kitchen duty. Instead, I started working with a landscaping crew. We worked the grounds of the camp and picked up trash along Interstate 70. The prison let us drive John Deere Gators around the unit to do our work. For the trash detail on the interstate, they let me drive a truck out to the highway and back, dropping people off and picking them up.

The first few days I got to drive the truck, I felt like myself again. Everything in prison is designed to knock you down, to dehumanize you, to let you know how low you really are. Once I climbed behind the wheel of the truck without an officer sitting beside me, I felt like a man again. I had a sense of freedom I had not experienced since Andrew Collins had jumped in my face in Benton Harbor three years earlier. The sun came out and the weather warmed up for a couple of days, which made me feel even better.

My little taste of freedom, however, began to feel like a tease, like the prison held real freedom just out of my reach. Even though I could drive around and do my work without supervision, I remained an inmate in the federal prison system. Some of my old thoughts came back about how I didn't deserve to be here, how I was innocent. If not for Collins's lies, I really would be free back home in Benton Harbor, spending time with my son and working my car wash.

The more I thought like this, the more I began to see that the truck I drove presented an opportunity. Nothing could stop me from driving right past the crew I was supposed to pick up on Interstate 70 and driving straight on home. At first, this fantasy was just a crazy thought that ran through my head. Before long, though, all I could think about was leaving. Who was going to stop me?

When the thoughts of leaving got really bad, I went back to my room and opened up my Bible. I read the story of Joseph. Like me, he'd been put in prison because of someone's lies. He hadn't done anything wrong, but they locked him up and forgot about him. Then he had a little taste of freedom and the hope that he was going to go free soon. But his hope didn't come true. Joseph nearly gave up, but God had him stay put, and that's what I sensed he was telling me. Back in Milan he had told me to let it go, and now he was telling me to stay put. I opened up to him and prayed, *God, I'm tired. Nothing I've done has worked. God, it's your way. It's your way, not mine.*

I stopped thinking about driving away.

Even though I'd had a real breakthrough with God, I still had not become involved in chapel. I don't know why. I guess I didn't want to make a big show of my relationship with God or make promises I couldn't keep. Instead, I just read my Bible and prayed and sought God.

The chapel at the camp was different from most chapels in one big way. Ron Isley, the founding member of the Isley Brothers, was one of the leaders. He was an inmate because of tax problems. Music is my passion, but even knowing Ron Isley was there wasn't enough to get me going. But then I got word that they needed someone to play bass and piano for the chapel band. Since I'd taught myself to play both during my time in Milan, I volunteered to play the bass. Before long they put me in charge of all the sound, the setup, recording the service, everything. Working in music again made it easier for me to stay put and be patient.

The only real downside to the camp was the mandatory drug program in which every inmate was supposed to participate. Right after I arrived I met with the counselor who ran the program. He told me straight out that I had to be a part of this program to stay in the camp. I refused. "I'm not going through any drug program because I don't have an issue with drugs."

"But you have a drug case. That means you have to take the program," the counselor argued.

"I don't have a drug case," I said.

"That's not what your record says."

"I don't."

"Anybody who was caught using or selling drugs has to take this class. It is a requirement by law," he said.

"Yeah, well, I'm not taking it. I have never done any drugs and I didn't sell any drugs. I hate drugs, so I ain't taking any drug rehab class."

"But it's the law!"

"I don't care. I'm not taking it. You can send me to the hole if you want, but I am not taking that class."

"All right. So be it," the counselor said, and the meeting was over.

About three weeks into my stay in the camp, I got up as if I were at home and went to work. I drove a group of guys out to the highway and dropped them off, then came back to the camp to do a little mowing. Even though it was early February, we'd had enough warm days that some weeds were sticking up. I drove the truck over to the shop to pick up a zero-turn mower, which I planned to use between a couple of the cottage houses that made up our housing units. I got out of the truck and heard the camp intercom crackle. "126945040, report to the warden's office." In prison you don't have a name. You have a number, and this one was mine.

My heart sank. All my appeals had been denied, so I knew they weren't calling to give me good news. *Has to be the fights,* I thought. *Those guys back at Milan finally spilled their guts about how I beat 'em up, and now I'm fixing to go to the hole.* I couldn't think of any other reason the warden might want to see me. It had to be the fights back at Milan. *My past has finally caught me.*

If I wasn't about to be sent to the hole for fighting at Milan, I figured it had to be my argument with the drug counselor. I'd even told him he could send me to the hole when I refused to take his drug class. Maybe he had called my bluff. Or maybe they were going to send me back to Milan or, worse, across the street to USP, all because I made a big deal about not taking the drug class. Either way, this was going to be bad.

Since nothing good could come out of my going to see the warden, I ignored the intercom and kept on working. I figured if they really needed me, they knew exactly where I was. They could send a truck out here and get me. I wasn't going to them. I mowed for a while and then took one of the Gators out to pick up some trash around the camp. When I was finished, I hauled the vehicle back to the shop and headed back toward Interstate 70 in my truck to pick up my crew. All the while the voice over the intercom kept saying, "126945040, report to the warden's office."

I kept ignoring it. The timing for this setback could not have been worse. I was finally in a good place spiritually and emotionally and even physically. If I had to spend the next six or seven years in a federal prison, I might as well spend it here. Working on a landscaping crew wasn't my dream job, but at least I got to be outside and I had some degree of freedom. Plus I got to work with the musicians in chapel, including the original Isley brother. I did not want to lose all of this to some stupid mistakes I made when I let my hate and anger at the cop who put me here boil over.

My crew unloaded the trash they'd collected and threw it in a Dumpster. By now it was around three in the afternoon. All through the drive back from the highway and over to the Dumpster, I felt sick to my stomach. I knew I was going to have to respond to the warden's summons sooner or later, and the time was now. With my work finished I went back to my unit. The first guy I saw said, "Hey, they've been calling you all day. You should probably go see what they want."

"Yeah, I'm fixing to," I said. But instead of heading straight to the office, I went back to my room and changed clothes. I figured if I was going to the hole, I didn't want to go in clothes covered with dirt and grass. There wasn't time for a shower, but I wished there was. It might well be my last chance to shower for a few weeks. *Oh well, time to face the music,* I thought and headed straight to the warden's office.

When I walked in the door, the warden asked me a strange question. He said, "Where would you go if you were released today, tomorrow, or six months from now?"

Release? Why is he asking me about release? I sort of shrugged my shoulders and said, "I guess to my grandma's house."

"I need an address," he said. I wondered why. Then he started writing things down in a ledger book. After a few moments he looked up at me and said, "I guess you were right." The fax machine beeped. He reached over, took the piece of paper from it, and handed it to me. "You have fifteen minutes to vacate the premises," he said.

Wait? What? I read the paper. It was an order from Judge Bell saying my conviction had been overturned and I needed to leave the prison premises immediately. I looked up at the warden. He showed no emotion at all.

"Really! This says what I think it says?" I asked.

"You have fifteen minutes to gather your belongings and go," he said to me like a landlord evicting someone for not paying their rent. "If you need anything from your room, you need to go get it now." He then handed me a one-way bus ticket to Benton Harbor by way of Indianapolis. There was no apology over my wrongful conviction. No "good luck to you." No nothing. It was basically a vibe that said, "You're trespassing and you have to leave."

"Man, I don't need *nothing*!" I said and headed toward the door. I walked outside and yelled, "Thank you, Jesus! Thank you, Jesus!" I knew this was nothing I or any man had done. The appeals court had thrown out every one of my lawyer's requests for my release. Humanly speaking, I should not have walked out of these gates for another six or seven years. The only explanation for my release was God. The timing also had his hands all over this. The day was February 4, 2009, my son's fourth birthday.

I nearly danced out of the prison and down the sidewalk toward the street. I wasn't just free. My conviction had been overturned. I was an innocent man. I didn't have a parole officer to report to or probation to keep. I had just been handed my life back. Hallelujah! Praise Jesus! All the way down the walkway and out through the front gate of the camp I kept dancing and praising God. Then I reached the street and realized, *Oh geez, I don't have a ride. Where am I gonna go now?*

I walked to the end of the street, trying to figure out how I was going to get to the bus stop when I saw one of the officers in a prison van. He'd been out getting gas. When he saw me, he said, "I can run you up to the bus station right now. No problem." Word had spread among the officers that my conviction had been overturned.

By the time the bus left Terre Haute and made the eighty-mile drive to Indianapolis, it was starting to get late. I got off the bus in Indy because my oldest brother, Kornell, lives there. I wanted to see my family and let them know what had happened instead of riding a bus all through the night. Since I did not have a phone of my own or money to use a pay phone (the prison gave me a bus ticket and nothing else when they set me free), the woman at the bus line main window let me use their phone. Kornell was surprised to hear my voice.

"Zookie? Hey, bro, what's up?" he said.

"I need you to come get me."

"What? Come get you? Where you at?"

"I'm in Indy at the bus station next to the football stadium. They let me go today. I'm a free man. The judge overturned my conviction."

"Nah, I'm not going to come get you. You had to have busted out of jail," Kornell said.

"I didn't bust out. They let me go," I said.

He still didn't believe me. "Where are you?"

I told him again, "I'm at the bus station in downtown Indianapolis. It's right across from the Colts' football stadium."

"How . . ." Then he said, "Hey, the phone you're calling from isn't a prison phone." He had just noticed the caller ID.

"I told you they let me out."

Kornell's voice started getting louder. "Zook! Where you at? You left that place for real?"

"Look, man, are you going to come get me or not?"

"Zook, man, I don't know. What's the number where you are right now?" Kornell wanted to call me back to make sure I was telling him the truth, because he still didn't believe me.

I asked the lady who'd let me use the phone if I could receive a call. She told me that normally they didn't allow it, but given the circumstances, she would. I gave Kornell the number, and he called back immediately. When he heard the lady say "Bus station" and then hand the phone to me, he nearly went crazy.

"What are you doing at a bus station?" he yelled. "You have over six years left. There's no way you should be out of that prison."

"I'm telling you I am free as a bird. I'll show you the paper when you get here. Now come get me!" Spending my first free night in a bus station was not what I had in mind when I danced out of the prison a few hours earlier.

"All right, I'm on my way," Kornell said.

I sat down and waited for him. And waited. And waited. An hour passed. I started to wonder if I should just get on the bus to Benton Harbor. Then the lady at the desk called my name. "There's a phone call for you," she said.

It was Kornell. The first thing he said was, "Where you at?"

"Bro, are you kidding me? I told you I'm at the bus station in Indy. Are you coming to get me or not?" I said, more than a little angry with him.

"You for real, ain't you?" he said. "They for real let you out of there."

"Yes. I told you I was. I'm at the bus station and I'm ready to get out of here. Dude, I can't even talk to you anymore. Here, talk to the lady and then come get me or I'm getting on the bus right now."

I gave the phone back to the woman. She spoke to my brother for a short time and then said to me, "He's on his way right now."

Twenty minutes later Kornell pulled into the bus station. When he saw me, his eyes got wide. He couldn't believe what he was seeing. He ran over and hugged me and said, "Zookie, I thought you were playing a joke on me."

"I told you I was here," I said. Even as I said this I noticed Kornell's eyes darting around like he expected the police to pull up at any moment. I pulled out the letter. "Here, read this," I said.

After Kornell read it, he looked up at me in shock. "You're free!"

"Yeah man. I'm free."

14

FACING THE CONSEQUENCES ONCE AND FOR ALL

Andrew

"Where are you going?" my three-year-old daughter asked as I stood in the kitchen dressed in a suit and tie.

I crouched down to her eye level and said, "Daddy has to go to court in Grand Rapids."

She threw her arms around my neck and cried, "Daddy, don't go!"

Tears welled up in my eyes. I wanted to tell her everything was going to be okay and I'd be back soon, but I couldn't. I could not lie to my daughter. "I have to go, sweetie. I don't have a choice."

"No, Daddy, don't go," she sobbed. "Don't leave me."

Believe me, I did not want to leave her. She'd never cried like this when I left the house. Everyone knew she was a daddy's girl, but this was out of character even for her. *She knows,* kept running through my head.

Finally I managed to extricate myself from her grip around my neck, and her grandma pulled her into her arms. I kissed my daughter goodbye and walked out the door wondering if I would ever kiss her in this kitchen again. My wife and I climbed into our car for the drive to Grand Rapids for my appointment in Judge Bell's courtroom. We pulled out of our driveway on the morning of January 26, 2009, not knowing when, or if, I'd be back.

Because I planned to plead guilty to the charges against me, I didn't have a trial per se. I appeared before Judge Bell to formally enter my plea. I'd been in his courtroom many times before, but this was the first time I noticed how everything was designed to intimidate the accused. The high ceilings and the judge sitting above the proceedings made me feel very, very small. Then I heard the words ring out, "The United States of America versus Andrew Collins." *The United States of America—the entire country—now stands against me,* I thought. I could hardly bear it.

After reading the charges against me and explaining my case, Judge Bell said with a cold tone, "Andrew, how do you plead?"

"Guilty, your honor."

"Have you been offered anything in return for a guilty verdict?" Judge Bell asked.

"No, your honor," I said. This was the truth. The proffer was not a substantiated offer. There was the understanding that my sentence might be reduced for my cooperation, but no deal had been struck.

"Can you give factual evidence for your guilty plea?" he asked. Frank, my attorney, had explained this ahead of time. I could not just say "guilty." The court had to make sure I understood the charges against me.

"Yes, your honor, I can."

"Well, tell me the circumstances of your case," the judge said. "You have pleaded guilty to possession with intent to deliver. Just who were you delivering to?"

"I did not sell the drugs and I did not deliver them to people," I said.

"Then how did you distribute them?" he asked.

"I kept the drugs in a locked container in my office. I used them as evidence, usually to attain a search warrant. When I needed them for this purpose, I packaged them and delivered them to the drug lab, where they were tested and then destroyed. So I guess you could say I delivered them to the person doing the testing," I explained.

"Don't you think that's stretching the 'delivery' piece a bit?" Judge Bell said with a tone that told me he was looking for more. *Delivery* meant delivery for sale, not carrying them down the hall of the police station. I got the feeling he wanted me to admit to something more than I had done or this whole proffer might come right off the table.

"No, your honor, because this is what I did."

He paused long enough to make me feel very uncomfortable. Finally he said, "So just to clarify, you carried the drugs to a lab, where they were tested and destroyed?"

"Yes."

"Okay. Your plea is accepted." He then read off the sentencing guidelines for the charges against me. The mandatory minimum was five years. The maximum was something like twenty or twenty-five years. It could have been seventy-five for all I know. All I remember was thinking it was a really long time, which made me very thankful I had cooperated with the FBI and prosecutors the past few months. Frank assured me the maximum was not a possibility. He hoped to secure something below even the minimum.

Once my plea was accepted, I expected to go home, still on bail, until my sentencing hearing. But the prosecutor would not have it. He stood and read a part of the federal statute covering guilty pleas to drug offenses. According to the letter of the law, when a guilty plea is entered, the defendant "shall be remanded to custody." Frank argued that the judge had discretion in such cases, that the law did not mean I had to be taken into custody immediately. The two went back and forth, arguing over the meaning of the word *shall*. In the end, Judge Bell agreed with the prosecutor.

When he made the announcement, I heard my wife gasp from the back of the courtroom. Federal marshals then led me to a holding cell, from which I was transported to the Kent County Jail in Grand Rapids. Although my formal sentencing hearing was scheduled for June, my imprisonment had already begun.

Since I was an ex-cop, the Kent County Jail didn't quite know what to do with me. They did not want to put me in with the general population in case someone recognized me. I might well run into someone I had put behind bars, and if I did, things might get ugly. Not knowing what else to do with me, they placed me in solitary confinement for my own protection. For two days I spent twenty-three hours a day alone in a cell, cut off from all outside contact. They let me out only for meals, which I ate by myself, and exercise, which consisted of a solitary walk around the unit.

The first day I had to make a decision whether to walk or stand in line to use one of the few pay phones available. I opted for the latter because I needed to talk to my wife. Given how rocky the past year had been, I did not know what to expect when we finally spoke. Even before our world collapsed, we seemed on the path to divorce. My being locked up could have been the clean break she needed. Not that I would have blamed her. After all, I'd brought this nightmare on her. No one would fault her if she opted for a fresh start without me rather than putting her life on hold for the next five years or more.

These thoughts ran through my head when I finally got to the phone. Making a phone call from jail is not an easy process. You have to call collect, and the person on the other end has to agree to set up an account to cover the costs. I think that's why a lot of men and women in prison never talk to anyone on the outside. I let out a sigh of relief when my wife agreed to accept the charges. Looking back, I had no reason to think she might refuse the call, but your mind plays tricks on you when you're behind bars.

I was relieved just to hear the sound of Krissy's voice. Then she said something that gave me the strength to face whatever lay ahead. "I'm fighting for us," she said. "We're in this together. Wherever you go, I got you."

Hope filled my heart. I knew we were going to make it now.

＝＝＝

Over the next few months the feds moved me every few weeks or even every few days from one county jail to another. Some places put me in solitary; others turned me out with the general population. I stayed busy reading. I read my Bible a lot. I also read Rick Warren's *The Purpose Driven Life*. My uncle gave me a copy of Chuck Colson's *Born Again,* which recounts not only his time in Washington but also his time in a federal prison because of Watergate. The book helped prepare me for what I faced. Thanks to Colson's book, part of me looked forward to seeing how God might use me behind the walls.

Because I wanted God to work through me in prison, I decided to be truthful and not hide from my past. I did not advertise that I was an ex-cop, but if someone asked, I admitted the truth. I also freely admitted I was guilty, which was pretty much a novelty in jail. When I was bouncing from jail to jail, surrounded by guys who were awaiting either their trials or their sentencing, I heard people talk about how innocent they were and how the cops had framed them. When they looked at me, I always said, "Not me, man. I did it. I'm guilty." Sometimes guys came up to me when it was just the two of us and admitted they were guilty too. However, I also met guys on the inside who truly were innocent but had been convicted anyway. That really bothered me. I hoped I had never put an innocent man behind bars.

From the start, my grandmother wrote me letters constantly. She reassured me she was praying for me and for the judge who was going to decide my final sentence. Her letters cheered me up. I noticed, however, that some of the guys I got to know never received any mail. I asked my grandmother to write to one of them and she did. He was so excited to get her letter. He wrote her back, thanking her for her letter. Then he asked if she would write to his wife, who was also behind bars. It's funny. Before I was locked up, I looked at the people I arrested as bad people who deserved whatever they got. Now I saw that most were just like me: decent people who'd made some really bad decisions for which they were paying the consequences.

My grandmother wrote to the man's wife and kept writing to him. By the time I was finally released, she was writing to many inmates. She still has that letter-writing ministry today. More people should do the same. Reading a letter from outside the walls gives inmates a brief taste of freedom.

I wanted to live a consistent life behind bars and be the man I was now striving to be. However, that wasn't always easy. I lived in the general population in the Mecosta County Jail for a couple of months. There I met a young guy from Detroit who was maybe nineteen years old. He'd been caught with a bunch of drugs. All day every day he screamed out rap lyrics at the top of his lungs from a nearby cell. When he wasn't rapping, he was being obnoxious in other ways. He rubbed me the wrong way until one day I just exploded. I was trying to get some sleep when he decided to scream some more rap lyrics. I got up, walked over to his cell, got in his face, and told him in no uncertain terms what I thought of him.

When I got back to my cell, the Holy Spirit got up in my face. God opened my eyes to see that this nineteen-year-old kid put on his tough front because he was scared to death. The last thing he needed was someone like me making life even harder for him. The next day I went to him and apologized. After that we became friends until we were sent on to other jails.

In June 2009 I finally had my sentencing hearing. This time I came straight from a county lockup. Instead of a suit and tie, I wore an orange jumpsuit with shackles hanging from my belly and chains running to my hands and feet. My hair was long and shaggy because I hadn't had a haircut since they locked me up five months earlier. My family was there as well as my pastor and some friends from church. I hated that they had to see me like this.

The hearing began with a report from the pre-sentence investigation committee. A woman spoke for the committee. She recommended I be given a sentence of fifty-eight months—two months less than the mandatory minimum. I couldn't help but think, *Gee, thanks. All those proffer meetings with the FBI for a whole two months.*

But then the prosecutor walked over to my lawyer and whispered something in his ear. Frank smiled, then went up to the judge and informed him that a 5K1 agreement had been reached. That agreement freed the judge to give me a lesser sentence. Frank then took his place beside me and recounted to the court all the ways I had cooperated with the FBI and the prosecutor's office. The prosecutor also made a statement agreeing with the 5K1.

Then it was Judge Bell's turn to make a statement.

Judge Bell looked angry when he first began to talk. He refused to even look at me as he spoke. "What this man did tears at the very fabric of our society," he said.

My immediate reaction was, *Oh, come on, man. That's a little extreme, don't you think?*

He continued, "One of the major differences between the United States and many other countries is the bond of trust between the citizens and those who enforce our laws. Here people are supposed to be able to trust the police, and this man has violated that trust."

Wow, I thought, *he is absolutely right. I did far more damage than I ever imagined. I did tear at the fabric that holds our society together.*

Judge Bell went on to speak of how I had broken the trust citizens have with police departments and judges and prosecutors and everyone else entrusted with upholding the law. I braced myself for what was going to come next.

Even though Judge Bell seemed angry, a couple of things he said made me think that he in some way understood why I did what I did. When he spoke of the people against whom I had committed my crimes, he referred to them as "nefarious people" and "not upstanding citizens." He also affirmed the fact that even though I attained my search warrants illegally, when I carried them out, these same nefarious people were caught with drugs. He chided me for "cutting a very, very critical corner in the criminal justice process," and I agreed. But in my mind I still wanted to believe that my real crime was being overzealous and lazy, which led to the corner cutting. I came away from Judge Bell's courtroom believing he felt the same way, even though that was me reading too much into his words.

After chiding me for my crimes, Judge Bell's tone softened. Before pronouncing my sentence, he commended me for the actions I'd taken since I'd been caught. He said, "This Court is reasonably satisfied that not only have we gotten your attention, but that you have made some choices mentally and spiritually and otherwise which, if followed, will probably keep you miles from doing this again." Even so, he sentenced me to thirty-seven months in prison with a fine of ten thousand dollars, which I was to pay to the city of Benton Harbor.

I was not thrilled that I was going to prison, and I had no idea where the ten grand was going to come from, but given all that had happened, thirty-seven months—including the five months I had already served—along with a fine was far better than what I had expected. My grandmother and my family and everyone else I knew had prayed the judge would show me mercy, and I believed he had. Proverbs 21:1 says, "The king's heart is in the hand of the Lord; he directs it like a watercourse wherever he pleases."

Immediately after my sentencing, my first stop was the processing center in Milan, Michigan, not far from Ann Arbor. They put me in with the general population, which made me more than a little nervous. I'd been there maybe a week when a new group came in. Two guys in the group looked familiar to me, and I to them. We sort of looked at one another from across the room, and then they began to whisper to each other. That's when it hit me. I knew these guys because I had investigated them in Benton Harbor for heroin sales. Right then I knew I was going to have a conversation I really did not want to have with someone in this place.

The whispering continued around me for the next couple of days. Guys all over the room looked at me in a different way. Finally, someone pulled me aside and asked, "Did you used to be a cop?"

I cringed but told the truth. "Yep. I was."

Other guys overheard the conversation, which brought them over to me. None of these guys were from Michigan. I didn't know how they were going to react to what I had just admitted.

To my surprise, one of them said, "Wow! Well, spill it. What'd you do that put you here?" Apparently crooked cops fascinated them. We talked for a long time. By the time I left Milan, these guys were my new best friends. They wished me luck on my way out the door. The two Benton Harbor guys did not have such a cheery disposition toward me. We never spoke, but looks were exchanged. I was glad I was leaving them behind.

My next stop after Milan was supposed to be a federal holding facility in Oklahoma City. However, when I stepped off the plane, an officer put a black *X* on my arm. They then placed me on a bus with a bunch of other guys with *X*'s on their arms. The bus headed southwest out of Oklahoma City.

We ended up in Chickasha, Oklahoma, at the Grady County Jail. I heard someone mumble something about "Shady Grady." It didn't take long to figure out what they were talking about. Walking into the Grady County Jail felt like stepping back in time to the Old West. They herded us into the facility like cattle and then had us sit in a gym while each of us went through the booking process. The temperature outside hovered around one hundred degrees, and the gym air-conditioning could hardly keep up. For a guy who grew up in northern Michigan, I was pretty miserable.

When it came my time to be booked, the guard processing me looked at his computer screen, then back up at me and said, "Oh." He looked down again, then back up and said, "Looks like we're gonna need to put you in a special housing unit."

I didn't ask what he saw. Inmates don't ask a lot of questions, especially in a place like Shady Grady. An officer then escorted me to a nurse's station. A large steel door behind the station opened, and I went into an eight-by-eight cell with a barred window that faced what looked like someone's yard. A raised concrete slab was apparently my bed even though it didn't have any kind of mattress or bedding or pillow. A toilet sat in the corner. The room didn't have a clock or books or anything except the barred window, concrete slab, and toilet. Clearly this was a punishment cell, but for me it was my special housing, where I had been placed for my own protection. They didn't even let me out for my meals. I spent all day, every day in that eight-by-eight box.

That first night I managed to fall asleep on the concrete slab. If you're tired enough, you can sleep on anything. When I awoke, everything looked exactly like it did when I fell asleep. I had no idea whether I'd been asleep eight minutes or eight hours.

When my meals came, I asked if I could call my wife. She had no idea where I now was. "Yeah, we'll get around to it," the officer said. I also asked for a Bible and anything else they might give me to read. All I had to do all day was stare at the concrete wall with no concept of the passing of time. *Is this how I'm going to spend the next three years?* I wondered. I shuddered at the thought.

On the third day in my eight-by-eight box, I went on a hunger strike. I decided I'd rather take my chances with the general population than lose my mind in this isolation cell where I was being punished for my own protection. The jail gave in and moved me to the medical ward. It was still isolation, but at least I had a shower and access to a pay phone. There was also a television that helped pass the time.

I ended up in a Level I prison in Miami, Florida, where I was to serve out my time. I had just gotten settled in when I was told I had to go back to Michigan to testify against my old partner, B. They took me by bus from Miami to Atlanta. Before I got on the plane in Atlanta, they put an *X* on my arm. I knew what it meant: my return trip to Michigan to testify against B would include a stopover at the Grady County Jail in Chickasha, Oklahoma.

After my two-week stay, when they put me on the bus to go to the Oklahoma City airport, I told one of the officers that I was never coming back to Chickasha. God, it seems, has quite the sense of humor. When we got to the airport, we learned that a snowstorm had hit Michigan and we were not able to fly. They loaded me back onto a bus, and back I went to Shady Grady.

Somehow, after testifying, I avoided a stopover at Grady County jail when they sent me back to Miami. I'd like to say I will never go back to Chickasha again, but at this point I've learned to never say never. I'm just thankful it was not my final destination.

15

TRYING TO PUT THE PIECES BACK TOGETHER

Jameel

I was pretty much in shock throughout the ride from Indianapolis to Benton Harbor. As I watched the road go by outside the bus window, my mind had trouble processing that I was really free. I wasn't on probation. I wasn't on parole. I was free with no charges against me. My family back home in Michigan was not as surprised as me because they had followed the Andrew Collins case in the news. By the time I walked out of the Terre Haute prison, the cases of a lot of people he'd arrested had already been dismissed. But I had no idea any of that was going on.

After reuniting with my family at my grandma's house, my twin brother, Jamal, told me, "That cop who arrested you, you know he's in prison now."

I nearly fell over when I heard those words. "What?" I said.

"Oh, yeah, he's in prison. They caught him with some dope and stuff in his locker. He pleaded guilty to everything."

"For real?" I said. This was the craziest thing I'd ever heard.

Jamal nodded his head. "Yeah, bro, for real. That's why they let you out. They've been dropping charges and letting a lot of people out that he arrested."

Now the letter from Judge Bell made sense. No one, not the warden or Judge Bell in his letter, had explained why my charges had been dismissed. As far as I knew, the store security tape had finally shown up. This was even better. The court had to throw out Collins's testimony against me, and since they didn't have any other evidence, my conviction was overturned. In my mind that proved what I had been saying all along. I was innocent. I later learned that not everybody believed me, even after I was released. Some members of my own family thought I'd been let out on a technicality.

Still, I didn't spend much time thinking about what people thought about me. I didn't have time for that. Now that I was out of prison, I had to figure out what I was going to do with my life. A couple of days earlier my plans for the next six-plus years of my life revolved around mowing the grass around the prison housing units. Thinking about my long-term future didn't do me any good in prison because it was too far away to worry about. The only real long-term plan I'd ever made was to hunt down and kill the cop who had put me away. Thanks be to God, I didn't want to do that anymore, but I also didn't know what I wanted to do. Music had always been my passion, and I got to do a lot with it both in Milan and Terre Haute. I'd learned to play several instruments and to operate equipment in a recording studio. I'd planned to do more with music in Terre Haute. But now, all of a sudden, I was out.

Jamal told me I could stay with him for as long as I needed while I figured things out. And I had a lot to figure out. For the first couple of months I didn't do much other than hang out with my family. I think I was in shock.

About two weeks after my release, a lawyer contacted me about a federal lawsuit he planned to file against the city of Benton Harbor and Andrew Collins. He invited me to meet with him, which I was glad to do. The meeting didn't last long, maybe half an hour. The attorney explained the reasoning behind the suit. The way he told it, the chief of police and others in authority either knew or should have known what was going on with Collins. Because they didn't control one of their officers, my civil rights had been violated, which was the basis of the suit.

I was on board right from the start. Three years of my life had been taken without so much as an apology. But it wasn't just the time they'd taken. Before my arrest I was a month or two away from opening my own car wash in nearby Michigan City, Indiana. My test run of the location in the fall of 2005 had been a big success, and I had a partner who was going to help me get the car wash off the ground. Three years later, he'd moved on without me.

I could handle losing the business. What I could not get back was the time I'd lost with my son. I was supposed to meet him for the first time when Collins arrested me. The moment my ex heard I'd been arrested, she took off and took my son with her. I hadn't heard from her since.

Someone told me she'd moved to Alabama. Then I heard she was in Fort Wayne, Indiana. Wherever she was, I still hadn't seen my son, and I had no idea when I ever would. I tried really hard not to be bitter and angry over it all. That stuff had nearly killed me in prison. I didn't need to go back down that road now. But, you know, right is right, and someone needed to make this right.

In my first meeting with the lawyer, he handed me a file with all the information about Collins. Reading it was like watching the movie *Training Day*. I had been suspicious of police my whole life. There's not a lot of trust between the police and the community in towns like Benton Harbor. What little trust I'd had disappeared when I was arrested for carjacking at the age of fifteen. The cop who took me in was actually dating one of my aunts at the time. Or had dated her. I think they'd had problems, which made me think he was getting back at her through me. I thought that was pretty messed up, but then I started reading the Collins file. Wow! That dude took things to a whole new level. I couldn't believe the stuff he'd done and how long he did it without getting caught.

When I finished reading about Collins, I figured the lawsuit was a slam dunk. So did the lawyer. That's part of the reason I didn't do a lot for the first couple of months after I got out. The attorney didn't tell me when he thought the lawsuit might be settled, but from the way he talked, it sounded like it could happen quickly. I figured before I jumped into any kind of job, I should wait to see what happened with the lawsuit. Who knows? Even after the lawyer took out his 30 percent, I might have enough to do something like the car wash. What I really wanted to do was build my own recording studio. If the lawsuit gave me enough money, I might actually get to do that.

The biggest question I faced right after I got back to Benton Harbor was how I was going to get around. I knew for sure I was never going to get into a car with anyone except maybe my grandma and my brothers. Other than that, no way. To this day I still won't get into a car with anyone I'm not absolutely positive is completely clean. Before I'd get into a car with someone I don't know, I'd need a drug-sniffing dog to go through it and make sure the whole thing is clean. Then I'd have to pat the person down and do a thorough search to make sure they weren't up to anything illegal. The same is true of the houses I go into. Call me paranoid, but I've been burned twice and robbed of years of my life that I can never get back. I'm not going to be in the wrong place at the wrong time ever again. No way!

Before I went off to prison, I had a car. I last drove it the morning of my arrest when the cop told me to park it until I took care of my unpaid tickets. When I got home my old car was right where I'd left it, but it wasn't in the same shape. Someone had busted out one of the windows. Leaves and snow had blown in and covered the inside. The tires had all gone flat and dry-rotted away. The engine didn't even turn over, much less start after sitting idle for three years.

With no job and no settlement money from the city, I didn't have the cash to buy another car. I had no choice but to try to get my old car up and running again. Some friends paid me to help fix up their cars, and I used the money to slowly repair my own car. The first thing I did was go down to the junkyard and get a new window. Then I cleaned out the inside and detailed it. I bought new tires and then worked on the engine. Slowly but surely it started to look and act like a car again. A few months after I got home, I had wheels again. I sure was glad because I was tired of walking everywhere I went.

When it became clear the lawsuit wasn't going to be settled anytime soon, I started looking for a job. I've never been afraid of hard work, so I figured I could find a job pretty quickly. However, finding a good job around Benton Harbor can take some time. I put together a résumé and started sending it out. That's when I discovered another lasting consequence of my false arrest. When I listed my work experience, I had a three-year gap from the time I was in prison. Companies took a look at that, and red flags went up. Even though I explained the situation to them, most places didn't want to hire someone who had spent time in a federal prison, even if his conviction was thrown out later.

After running into a few brick walls, I went to a temp agency who placed me in a die-casting plant part time. At first they scheduled me only on weekends. I really needed a full-time job. You can only sleep on your brother's couch for so long, but I took the job because I didn't have a lot of other options. When I proved to be a good worker, they moved me to a full-time shift. However, they paid only $8.50 an hour. No one can live on that, but I kept working there because I needed something.

I also got a job at a body shop. Every day I worked an eight-hour shift at the die-casting plant and then went straight to the body shop, where I worked another couple of hours. I also worked for a while as a bouncer at a club, but I got tired of that pretty fast. I did not enjoy breaking up fights.

After ninety days, my probationary period at the die-casting plant ended. The company reviewed my file to see if they wanted to hire me permanently, which also meant a small raise. But then my boss called me into his office. He pointed to my file and said, "We can't hire you because you have a drug arrest."

"What are you talking about?" I said. I thought the court had cleaned up my record when they dismissed the charges against me. They hadn't.

"In 2006 you were arrested for selling crack," the manager said.

"Those charges were dismissed and that was supposed to have been taken off my record because I didn't do it," I replied.

"I don't know about any of that," he said, "but you have a drug arrest, and we can't hire anyone with a drug arrest on their record." That ended my days at the die-casting plant. When I walked out for the final time, I wondered how much more that false arrest was going to cost me.

I found another job right away at a company that did nickel and hard-chrome plating. If they knew about my arrest, they didn't seem to care. I cleared my probationary period and settled into the job. After I'd worked there awhile, I saved enough to get a place of my own and move out of my brother's house. Life finally started to feel normal again.

I still stayed pretty much to myself and remained extra cautious about where I went and who I was with. In a way I was a lot like I was in prison, only without the anger eating me up. God had set me free from that. He set me free not just from my anger but also from the prison itself, and for that I was eternally grateful. One thing I was not, though, was a churchgoer or even much of a God-centered person. I pretty much left God in prison. I guess I felt as though I didn't need him on the outside.

Life wasn't easy, but that's life in Benton Harbor. Life wasn't too easy for anybody I knew. But all in all, I was doing all right. I had never been a churchgoer, not after the negative experiences I had with church growing up, and I didn't really see a need to change now. God and I had been tight in Milan and Terre Haute, even though I wasn't that involved with chapel. I figured I didn't need church to consider myself a Christian. No, when it came to God, everything was basically the way it had been before I met Andrew Collins, and I saw no need to change that.

The main thing I did not have in my life that I really wanted was a relationship with my son. Two years after I got out of prison, I still had not seen him, but I wanted to. I wanted to see him more than anything, but I had no way of getting in contact with him. Then one day while I was still living with my brother, my ex showed up with my son. I don't remember if she called ahead of time or anything like that. I didn't even know she was back in town. She didn't stay long, just long enough to drop off my son and tell me he was mine for the summer. Then she left. It was a drop and dash. He didn't have any extra clothes with him or anything, but that didn't matter to me. We could buy clothes.

That first meeting was surreal for both of us. I was like, "Hi, I'm your dad." Even though he had never met me, he knew who I was because he'd seen pictures of me and heard about me. We made up for lost time pretty fast. The first thing I did was take him shopping for clothes and shoes and anything else he needed to live with me for a while. I was so happy getting to do this. I mean, that's the kind of things dads are supposed to do. When we got back to the house that first night, we played some video games and had fun together. I just wanted to get to know him, and I didn't know how much time I was going to have with him beyond this one summer.

Our first morning together I got up and made breakfast. I asked my son what he wanted to do that day. This whole dad thing was new to me. I wasn't too sure what a six-year-old might want to do. We ended up going over to my older brother Richard's house. I wanted my son to meet the rest of his family. My cousin David was also there.

After hanging out at my brother's house for a while, my son and I went for a walk. David came along. We took off down Empire Street. I planned to keep walking and head back toward home. But my son noticed a lot of people in Broadway Park and wanted to check it out and see what was going on. I was a little surprised people were actually in the park. The last time I paid any attention to the park, it had been all grown over with weeds and trees. No one had used it for a long time. But apparently someone had cleaned it up. On this day it looked like everyone in town was there, so we decided to check it out. I had no idea who the group was. If I had, I probably would have kept walking down the street.

16

BROADWAY PARK

Andrew

My journey home from federal prison began on an August day in 2010 with a prison van dropping me off at a mall across the street from the Miami bus station. Someone had made a mistake when they printed my release orders. I had to leave the prison at one o'clock in the afternoon, but the bus didn't leave until nine that night. When he dropped me off, the official warned me, "If you screw up while you're waiting for the bus, that's on you." I assured him I had no intention of screwing up.

After waiting eight hours for the bus, I embarked on a three-day bus ride. That's three days straight on a bus. Through the South. In the middle of August. There were no layovers where I could take a shower or sleep lying down or call my wife and let her know where I was. I spent the entire time on the bus. For entertainment I watched a mom and daughter drink for two days nonstop before they got off in Georgia or Tennessee. I guess they had made the trip before and decided the only way to survive was to self-medicate.

After three days on the bus, I still did not get to go

home. Before I could be released into the general population, I had to spend three months in a halfway house called KPEP, where I was required to take classes to prepare me for life on the outside. Most people there also spend this time looking for a job, but I had a job waiting for me thanks to a family friend. I still had to stay at KPEP though.

In my opinion this was a terrible idea. KPEP is in the heart of Benton Harbor, which put me right back at ground zero. More than that, since KPEP is a transitional facility for people getting out of prison, there was a very good chance that at least some of the guests might be people I'd put behind bars. I went to the administration and pleaded my case, arguing that this wasn't the best place for me. Eventually my time at KPEP was cut down to six weeks. Then, at last, I was able to return to my home in a town not far from Benton Harbor.

I went right to work at a farm east of town. I worked alongside migrant workers boxing jalapeño peppers as well as standing over a conveyor belt and culling bad tomatoes. I was paid minimum wage. It wasn't my dream job, and my family couldn't have survived on what I made, but the pay was a lot more than I contributed to the family while I was in prison. Unfortunately, our financial obligations also included the $10,000 fine Judge Bell had ordered me to pay the city of Benton Harbor. I had to write regular checks to the federal court system, who then sent the money to the city. Ten grand was equal to a loan for a decent used car, which is why I drove an old car my mom gave us. The car had almost three hundred thousand miles on it and the bottom was nearly rusted through, but it got me to work and back, and for that I was very grateful.

Now that I was out, I joined my wife and daughter at a church called Overflow. We actually had started going there just before I went to prison. The church met in the movie theater at a mall on the outer edge of Benton Harbor, not far from where my wife worked. Krissy met the pastor at the mall and then seemed to run into him at least once a week. Every time she saw him, he invited us to church. During my time in prison, Pastor Brian (this pastor was also named Brian) wrote to me regularly. The church also helped my wife and daughter get by while I was away. After my release we not only started going to the church, but I also volunteered for the tech team.

As strange as it may seem, during my first few months back home, I felt that God still wanted to use me in some way in Benton Harbor. Krissy wasn't so sure. Benton Harbor and the surrounding area are pretty small, so I knew it was only a matter of time before I started running into people I'd put in prison. It didn't take long at all. I was nervous about how things might go down when someone actually confronted me, but the initial encounters left me pleasantly surprised.

The first guy I met acted mad at first, but he lightened up when I owned up to everything and apologized for what I had done to him. We both knew he should have been thanking me, because if I'd gone by the book, he'd still be in prison. At one point I smiled and said, "Come on, man, we both know you were dirty."

"Yeah, Collins, but you were dirtier," he said with a laugh.

"Yeah, man, you're right," I said. I knew the worst thing I could do was minimize what I had done. God had convicted me that the best thing to do was own up to everything.

The next couple of reunions went about the same. Then I ran into people who had no intention of letting me off the hook. A few guys cussed me out, but I figured I deserved it. Thankfully, no one ever became violent with me or even seemed like they might. I started to relax a little bit. I wasn't dreading these reunions the way I did before I got back home.

After a month of working on the farm, I found a job at a discount tire store not far from our church. After working there a few months, I noticed that a man who'd stopped by just to put air in one of his tires was staring at me. Immediately I knew why. The longer he stared, the more the expression on his face changed. By the time he finished airing up his tires, he looked really, really mad. He came straight over to me and got up in my face and started spewing profanities. I could take that, but then he said he was going to come back with a gun and shoot the place up. That was my last week of work at the discount tire place. I did not want to put anyone else at risk because of me.

The confrontation at the tire store made me think that perhaps I should not work out in the open with the public. I found a job at a factory in town and tried to blend in. A few of the people I worked with recognized me. My face had been plastered all over the news, so they knew who I was and what I had done. But since I didn't work with anyone I had ever arrested, there were no angry confrontations—at least not at work.

I still ran into people from time to time at a grocery store or gas station. To keep these encounters to a minimum, I did my best not to spend a lot of time in the heart of Benton Harbor, where most of the people I'd put away lived. Krissy and I even discussed moving. We talked about moving south, maybe to Georgia or Tennessee or even Florida. As long as I didn't have to take a bus to get there, I was fine with any of these places. We also considered moving west, perhaps to Colorado or even California, any place far enough away where we could start fresh.

Deep down, though, I felt that God had something for me to do in Benton Harbor. When I became a cop, I wanted to make a real difference in my community. I'd made a difference, but not in the way I wanted. The desire to make a positive impact had not gone away. If I could find a way to be used by God in this town, then perhaps that might provide some sort of redemption for me. God had given me a strong story of how he can turn your life around and use your failures for his purposes, no matter how badly you mess up.

One day at work, while I was thinking about this, I came up with an idea to throw an outdoor block party at one of the parks in Benton Harbor. I thought it could be a first step for our church to build bridges to the community at large. Overflow was already a diverse church with people from all walks of life. On any given Sunday you were as likely to sit next to an executive as you were a homeless person.

I went to Pastor Brian with the idea, and to my surprise, he told me the church already held an annual event like that at Broadway Park, which had once been pretty run down. Organizers called it H3, which stood for Hoops,

Hotdogs, and Hip-Hop. A team from the church had cleaned the place up, hauling away a lot of brush and trash. I remembered how bad the park looked when I was a cop. By the time the team from Overflow finished their work, it was a pretty nice park with swings, a play area, and a basketball court.

When the time for H3 rolled around, I volunteered to run the snow cone machine as well as referee some of the basketball games. On the day of the event, I took my daughter along, but Krissy didn't attend. She still had serious reservations about how wise it was for me to do anything visible in town. She'd been with me during some of the confrontations I'd had, and they'd left her shaken. A lot of the people who had something against me had violent records. The question was not if one of these confrontations might turn violent, but when. Even so, I believed God had called me to Benton Harbor and he'd protect me while I was there.

I got into the flow of H3 and nearly forgot any reservations I'd had about coming. I felt more and more comfortable at the festival, until I saw the crowd begin to part like the Red Sea.

Jameel

If I hadn't had my son with me, I never would have walked down Empire Street that day. Even if I had, if my son hadn't been with me, I never would have walked into a park filled with people. And Broadway Park was packed. People were everywhere. When I saw the crowd I tried to keep moving down the street, but my son pulled on my hand, begging me like only a six-year-old can. "Please, please, Dad, can we go over there? I want to see what is happening."

This was only my second day with my son. I was not about to tell him no. My cousin Dave was with us too. We reached the edge of the park, and my son ran along on the grass, looking around very excitedly. I stayed right next to him, though I walked on the sidewalk. I watched the cars going by to make sure he didn't dart into the street. I also scanned the people in the park, looking for possible trouble. Old habits from prison die hard.

My son spotted the swings about the same time I saw the one man I never expected to see here: Andrew Collins. The moment I laid eyes on him, all the anger and hate I had felt in prison came rushing back. All of a sudden, nothing else mattered but doing what I had dreamed of doing for years. I grabbed my son and said, "Let's go." He probably protested and said he wanted to play. I don't remember if he did. Right then, all I wanted to do was get to Collins before he slipped away.

I was on the far side of the park from where Collins stood. My son and I took off walking, with Dave trying to catch up. I set my eyes on Collins and went straight toward him. I don't know if people saw the look in my eyes or what, but everyone got out of my way without my saying a word. Dave must have recognized Collins too, because he started talking in my ear, telling me to stop or not to do this or something like that. I don't know exactly what he said because I wasn't listening. This was my chance, my moment, and I was not going to let it pass. I knew what I was going to do, and neither Dave nor my son nor anyone else was going to stop me.

When I reached Collins, I stopped and stuck out my hand. I wanted him to know who I was before I did anything. "Remember me?" I said.

"Jameel McGee," he replied.

I knew what I had come here to do. This scene had played over and over and over in my head while I was in prison so many times it was as if it had already happened. But then, when he said my name, I hesitated. The moment I heard his voice I also heard another voice that was even louder. I recognized the voice, and I recognized the message. It was the same three words I'd heard in my prison cell in Milan: *Let. It. Go.*

Collins started talking. To be honest, I'm not sure what he said because I was having a conversation of my own. God was talking to me. It was only three words, but that was enough. *Let it go,* he said.

No, God. I can't let it go. If I don't do this right now, if I don't pay him back for what he did to me, how will I ever look anyone in this town in the eye again?

Let it go.

I argued with God. *I'm right here,* I said. *I have to do this.*

But God argued back. *Jameel, what are we doing here? Why are you doing this? We let this go in prison. That's how you got to come home. Remember how I set you free right after you turned loose of this anger? Why do you want to grab hold of it again? What is this going to do?*

No, God, no, I said. *Just let me do this and then I'll turn loose of everything again. I promise.*

As this battle was going on in my head and in my heart, I squeezed harder and harder on Collins's hand. I mean, I was really squeezing it hard. I had to because I was in pain. This was a battle, and it was all inside of me. I'd been out of prison for two years, and in those two years I had left God back in that prison. But today, in this park, he came and found me.

At one point I finally heard something Collins said about being a new person because of God and Jesus. And he apologized. I did hear that. That apology resonated with me. He wasn't ducking what he had done. He was owning up to it, which surprised me. By the time he apologized, I was breathing kind of hard. Man, this was a battle and it was rough. After he said he was sorry, I nodded toward my son and said something that had been boiling inside of me for a while. "Yeah, well, I need you to tell him why he missed out on three years of his daddy's life."

Even as I said this I heard God say very loudly, *Let me handle this. I got this. Let it go.*

Okay, God. This is yours. I'd be a fool to intervene now. I am not that man who wanted revenge. That man is dead and gone. God took him away in prison.

I was about to turn loose of Collins's hand and walk away when he opened his mouth and started talking again. He actually tried to compare his experience to mine by saying something about how he'd missed out on eighteen months of his daughter's life just like I'd missed out on three years of my son's life. That comment nearly pulled all the anger back. I mean, I got heated when I heard it. I was like, *Come on, God. Let me take just one shot at him. Please!*

And what's that going to solve? God replied. *Let it go.*

So I did, but not before I gave Collins a few choice words describing what I thought about his "sacrifice"!

Then I let go of his hand. The moment I did, I was free. The anger evaporated. God took it away just like that. I turned around and walked away, feeling lighter. This was my chance for revenge, but I let it go. I gave my thirst for revenge over to God, along with my anger and hate. And he set me free. I thought I had surrendered everything to God in my cell in Milan, and honestly, I had. But I had to have this moment with Collins in the park to be truly free.

It is one thing to say you have released something to God, but you cannot really know if you have until you are tested on it. This was my test. I nearly flunked, but God didn't let me. I thought I'd left him back in the prison, but he was right here, waiting for me at the very moment I needed him most. If he hadn't been, if I'd done what I wanted to do, then, man, my life might have been over.

When I left the park that day, I left behind everything I'd ever had against Andrew Collins. When I let go of his hand, I had truly forgiven him in my heart, but that doesn't mean I wanted to hang out with him or anything like that. I figured I'd never see him again, and I was fine with that.

Boy, was I ever wrong. After that day in the park, it seemed like everywhere I went, I saw Andrew Collins. I'd go into a store and see him coming out. We didn't speak, and I don't think he saw me, but I saw him. At Meijer. At Walmart. I'd be on my way home from work, and who would I see driving by in his car? Andrew Collins. It was like he was everywhere I went. I was glad I'd surrendered my anger to God in the park, because seeing him so often would have driven me crazy otherwise.

At one point I started second-guessing God. *Was I supposed to do something to him, Lord?*

Andrew

I walked away from meeting Jameel feeling like a failure, like maybe this whole idea of being reconciled to the community in a redemptive way was my idea, not God's. I felt stupid for taking my daughter to this event. The place wasn't safe. I didn't know what kept Jameel from taking a swing at me, but I was pretty sure he wanted to. If he had, what would my daughter have thought as she saw her father being knocked to the ground? What if this had escalated beyond Jameel and me? A riot could have broken out in Broadway Park. How could I have kept her safe? I couldn't have. Why did I ever think this was a good idea?

I did not tell Krissy about meeting Jameel. I couldn't. It's not that I wanted to hold anything back from her, but I didn't think sharing these details was beneficial for either of us. When I got home, I came to the conclusion that moving probably was the best idea for our family. If I could not be reconciled to this community, the best thing I could do for my wife and daughter and myself was to put as many miles as possible between us and Benton Harbor.

All this was still going through my head the next day when I went to church. Right before the service started, Pastor Brian said, "So H3 was pretty awesome, wasn't it?"

"Uh, yeah," I said in a tone that made it clear it was anything but awesome to me. Then I told him, "I had a bad encounter with Jameel McGee." However, when I said Jameel's name, I mispronounced it as Jamal.

Pastor Brian looked at me with a really strange look. "Really? That seems very odd. We just hired him down at the café." Overflow had an outreach coffee shop, café, and thrift store used as a job-training ministry.

"You did?"

"Yeah, so God's probably got something planned there. You two are probably going to cross each other's paths. You're going to need God to work this out."

I walked away thinking about what Pastor Brian had said. Our paths were going to cross. And God was going to have to work this out—but not in the way Pastor Brian expected. He hadn't hired Jameel. The church had hired his twin brother, Jamal. None of us discovered the misunderstanding for quite some time. By then God had worked something out, and he did it in a bigger way than anyone ever thought possible.

17

LOSING IT ALL—AGAIN

Jameel

When I walked out of Broadway Park with my son, I could not stop thanking God for saving me from myself. Then I told him goodbye and left God at the park. I didn't really intend to. It just sort of happened. I walked out of the park free from Andrew Collins. When I saw him again, and I kept seeing him a lot, I did not have to deal with all the old feelings of hate and anger I'd felt toward him. I was now free to get on with life, so that's what I did. Before that day in the park, God hadn't been a big part of my life except when I needed him, and nothing changed in that regard afterward.

My son spent the rest of the summer of 2011 with me. Then his mother showed up, and he went back with her to start the school year. I kept working at the nickel- and chrome-plating plant. I had no complaints about the work. It may not have been my dream job, but it was a job and it paid the bills.

The lawsuit against the city dragged on. About once a year I went to a meeting with the attorneys handling the case. They always talked as though a settlement was right around the corner, but then another year would go by without my hearing from them. They held meetings in 2010, 2011, and 2012. Every time it was the same story. Getting the settlement money would be really nice, but I wasn't counting on it. I had a job. I had a place to live. Life was all right. I wasn't living the dream, but it was a heck of a lot better than prison.

I went in to work one day in 2012 and found I'd been assigned to one of the assembly lines. I'd worked this one before. The work wasn't that hard. I spent the day putting metal caps on glass tubes that were about the size of ballpoint pens. I had to give each one a twist as I pushed down on it. Toward the end of the day, I picked up a tube and started to twist the cap onto it. As soon as I applied pressure, the tube shattered and half of it went straight through my right hand.

Immediately, I dropped to the floor as if I'd been shot. Blood spurted everywhere. The wound in my hand looked like a gunshot wound. I tried pulling the tube out, but half of it broke off inside me. One of my supervisors came running over and asked if I wanted to go to the hospital. At the time I thought I'd just cut my hand pretty badly, so I told him I'd finish my shift. I picked out the glass shards I could see, wrapped my hand in bandages, and finished the last few minutes of my shift.

Late that night I finally went to the hospital when the pain got to be more than I could take. I figured doctors would give me some stitches and a shot for the pain and send me on my way. Instead, I spent the night watching them digging pieces of glass out of me. Before they released me, they told me I could not return to work for at least a week. Since I'd been hurt on the job, the company paid my hospital bill, but I did not receive worker's compensation for the time I missed.

A week after my injury I had to go back to work in order to pay my bills. The doctor allowed me to return but warned me I could not do anything strenuous with my right hand. I already knew that. Even though my hand was wrapped tightly, it was swollen and hurt like crazy. Eventually I had to have a couple of operations on it, but those were months down the road.

My first day back at work, my supervisor put me on the line as though I'd never been injured. I told him I couldn't do it.

He said, "You're going to do it or you can go home!"

That was a no-brainer. I replied, "I'm going home, then, because I can't use my hand."

My boss had me come back a short time later and assured me the company was going to pay all my hospital bills and even the cost of physical therapy if I needed it. When I asked about worker's comp, the conversation pretty much ended. After working for the same company for three years, I was now out of work and had only one good hand.

As soon as the bandages came off my hand, I found another job. Since I had a good work record, another plant in town hired me right off. Then I reported to work and things fell apart. My hand looked like a balloon before I'd really even started working. The supervisor who was showing me what I was going to do looked down at it and said, "Whoa!" like he'd just seen a ghost or something. "Let me see that hand," he said. He took a close look, shook his head, and broke the news to me: "You can't work here with your hand in that shape."

"Why not?" I asked. "I'm cool with it."

"You might be, but we can't allow it. That hand makes you a liability. We can't hire you," he said.

The next day I received a call from the man who'd hired me. He broke the news I already knew: I could not come back. I had to find another job.

Over the next few months I found several jobs, one after the other. Some I kept for a few days before my hand started bothering me so much that I had to quit. More than one of the companies made it clear they wanted to keep me. If not for my hand, I could have worked for any of them as long as I wanted. But my hand always ballooned up, and that was the end of it. Eventually I found a job with a construction company that I kept longer than any of the others. I did a lot of physical work—hauling stuff, carrying buckets around, that sort of thing. Then one day my hand swelled up like a basketball and hurt so badly I could not lift a thing. That was the end of my construction career. Since I could not work a steady job, my bills started to pile up. Before long I lost my house and got my first taste of being homeless.

Thankfully, before things hit bottom I received some good news for once. The town lawsuit attorneys held another meeting toward the end of 2012. I expected to hear the same thing I'd heard each year. Not this time. The lawsuit had been settled to the tune of $13 million, which was to be divided among everyone who was a part of the lawsuit. The fifteen lawyers on the case took their 30 percent off the top. They presented us with a formula that had been worked out to decide how much everyone else received. The longer your prison sentence, the more money you received. Any money seized by civil forfeiture also played a part in the formula. My portion was $102,000. After taking out the attorney's fees, I came away with around $72,000.

The money could not have come at a better time. I moved into a new house and bought a car, a 1996 Cadillac Eldorado. I'd bounced around from job to job, but now I had the perfect solution. I found a location where I could finally open my own full-service car wash and detailing shop. I put $4,000 down on the building and sank another $2,000 into some equipment. When we opened I offered full detailing services, including waxes, interior shampoos, motor cleaning, scratch removal, small dent removal, and paint touch-ups.

Around that time I also started dating someone, and we moved in together. I felt as if I finally had my life together.

Then it all came apart.

The first crack came right after the settlement. I was driving down the road, not speeding, not doing anything illegal, and a state policeman pulled me over. I don't remember if he gave me a ticket or not, because the same thing happened the next day and the next and every day after that. Every time I left my house I got pulled over by the state police. The worst instance happened on my birthday. A state policeman pulled me over and threatened to arrest me for driving under the influence. He told me he thought I was high. I about lost it. "Dude," I told him, "I'm not high. I don't do that BS."

The patrolman went back to his car and then returned to inform me that he was going to take me in because my license had been suspended. That was news to me. He ordered me out of the car, but I did not budge. "My license is not suspended," I told him.

Eventually another patrolman showed up and I got out of the car. After they put me in the back of a squad car, they ran my license again. Just like that, it wasn't suspended any longer. "All right, let me out of this car so I can get on my way. It's my birthday and I have places to go."

"You're not going anywhere," the state patrolman said. "We're taking you in for driving while intoxicated."

I spent the rest of my birthday in jail for suspicion of DUI, even though I had not been drinking. They let me out the next day with no charges filed. But that didn't stop them from pulling me over on a daily basis. I checked around and discovered the same thing was happening to everyone who had received settlement money from the city of Benton Harbor. (You can draw your own conclusions from that.)

The cops stopped pulling me over only after I had a wreck that totaled my car. I was involved in a head-on collision right in front of my car wash. A fifteen-year-old girl with no license and no insurance was driving a car with illegal plates, and she hit me head-on. God protected me from any real harm. My Cadillac folded up around me, but I didn't have a scratch on me. I know God did that. Since I had only liability coverage, my insurance didn't cover the damage to my car. The other driver should have paid for it, but I knew I wasn't going to get anything from a fifteen-year-old girl.

The next blow came when I discovered that the man from whom I'd leased the building for my car wash didn't actually have the title to the building. The real owner lived in California and had put the building up for sale. The man with whom I'd worked made the deal with me because he needed to come up with some cash. By the time the dust settled, I'd lost my building along with all the money I'd put into the business. No building meant no business. Just like that I had to close.

After I lost my business, a body shop where I'd done some work in the past contacted me about working there. The manager asked me to do the same detail work on his customers' cars that I had offered at my car wash. We worked out a weekly pay rate. While it wasn't great, it was better than nothing, at least until I could figure out how to relaunch my own business. Unfortunately, the arrangement didn't last long. The body shop paid me late and sometimes not at all. I finally told the owner I was finished. He still owes me for two weeks' work. I chalked that money up as lost and went on my way. Even with the delay in starting my business, I should have been fine. I had most of the settlement money in the bank, enough to carry me over until I figured out my next move.

Then my new relationship fell apart. My girlfriend moved out and left town. I heard she'd moved to Atlanta. I didn't chase after her. I figured the best thing I could do was to chill for a little while before I made any other big decisions.

My plan didn't work, however. One afternoon my landlord called to tell me I was two months behind on my rent. I told him that wasn't possible since I'd set up an automatic payment through the bank. The only way I could have been behind would be if I was out of money, and I wasn't out of money.

Except I was.

When I went to the bank to find out why it hadn't sent my rent payments, I discovered my account was worse than empty. I had an overdraft of $500. Phone calls from Atlanta came right after that. One car dealer after another called about cars they said I'd purchased. At first I thought they had the wrong number. They didn't. Turns out my girlfriend took all my financial information and stole my identity before she left town. In two months she'd blown through every dime the city of Benton Harbor had given me as my part of the settlement.

Now I was completely broke. The identity theft destroyed my credit. I couldn't work because of my injured right hand. And my landlord evicted me. Just like that I found myself homeless and jobless.

It felt as though all this happened in a matter of days, even though it stretched out until the end of 2013. My life had spiraled out of control, and I did not know what to do next. My first response was to do what I did when I landed in the federal prison. I withdrew into myself. I pulled back from everything and everybody. It was just like I was back at the prison in Milan. I went into survival mode and didn't really trust anyone. I also didn't want to let people know what had happened to me. They had their business and I had mine, and I was more than happy to keep it that way. Someone advised me to go to the Social Security office and apply for disability. The office told me it was going to take a very long time to process my case. I was like, *Okay, cool, I'll take care of myself then.*

With no home to stay in and no job to go to, I spent my days walking up and down the less-traveled roads of Benton Harbor where I didn't see anyone and no one saw me. Most nights I slept in my brother's car. He left it unlocked when he got home from work, and I was out of it and back walking the streets before he left the next day. On some of the really cold nights or when I needed to take a shower, I went to my aunt's house, but I didn't do that very often because she didn't have any extra room. I stayed at the Salvation Army once, but I didn't go back because someone stole everything I had with me.

Those days were dark—darker than anything I'd ever experienced before, even darker than Milan. I just walked the streets all day. I didn't ask anyone for help because I felt ashamed. Everyone in town knew about the settlement money. The $13 million had been all over the news. I thought anyone who saw me in this condition would look down on me for throwing my money away so quickly. So I just kept walking down untraveled roads in the middle of winter in late 2013 and into 2014, which also happened to be one of the coldest winters ever. At night I put on all the clothes I had and curled up in the back seat of my brother's car. The next day I was back out, walking in the snow or sleet or whatever fell from the sky.

Without even realizing it, I found myself talking to God as I walked. It was like I was back on the track in the prison yard at Milan. I started pouring out my heart to him. *God, I'm home and I'm worse off than I ever was in prison.*

Why? What is going on? I thought about the people who'd betrayed me and I wanted to blame them, but the longer I walked the more I knew all this was on me. I was on the streets because of choices I had made, no one else. I admitted that to God. I told him I was here because of me. I thought back to the last time I walked along pouring out my heart to God. On that day I finally listened to God and let go of the anger that was eating me up inside. I didn't just let go of the anger, though. I made promises to God that day about how I was going to live for him and let him control my life. But the moment he set me free, I tossed all those promises aside, and this is where that decision left me: broken down, barely surviving, at the lowest of the lows.

God, I'm sorry, I prayed.

My auntie figured out what was going on when she saw me walking around her neighborhood every day. Without asking me, she made some phone calls on my behalf. One day she came to me and said, "You need to get some help."

"Nah, I'll be all right," I said. "I'm going to get it together."

She refused to take no for an answer. "I'm going to take you over to River-wood where they can help you." Riverwood Center is a mental health center in Benton Harbor.

"No. No way am I going there," I said.

My auntie persisted. "They can help you," she kept saying.

I didn't listen. Honestly, I didn't think anyone could help me at this point. I told her no firmly enough that she dropped it.

The winter got colder, cold enough that I went to my aunt's house to warm up and take a shower. She wanted to let me move in, but she had a house full of girls living with her at the time.* After I showered, my aunt told me she needed to meet her daughter somewhere and asked if I wanted to come along. I agreed to go. Her house was crowded, and a warm car sounded a lot better than the cold streets. We ended up at Riverwood. She told me that's where her daughter was. Then she asked if I had my ID on me. When I asked why, she

---

* After the girls all got their own places, I lived with my aunt for a short time before I got my own place.

told me she had to show them someone's ID to get in the door. She was lying, but I'm glad she was.

My aunt had already lined up an appointment for me with one of the doctors at Riverwood, Dr. Carter. I guess I could have left and not talked to him, but by this point I was tired of life. Dr. Carter sat down with me and opened our time together by saying, "You seem like a wreck, man. What's going on?" He didn't say it like a doctor but like a friend.

I let out a long sigh. "Yeah, I'm going through it. My auntie thought I should come here before it gets any worse." I then proceeded to let it all out.

When I finished, he jumped up and left the room, which struck me as odd. I saw him in the other room making phone calls. At first I thought he was calling the police or something. But when he came back, he explained he had been trying to find a place for me to stay. He couldn't reach anyone, which I told him was okay. Then he pulled forty dollars out of his pocket and pressed it into my hand, saying, "This is for clothes." He also gave me a number to call. "These people will get you some help," he said. I agreed to come back the next week and talk more with him.

Dr. Carter and the Riverwood Center connected me with Debra Mead, who worked for Michigan Rehabilitation Services (MRS). The agency helps people find jobs and get job training. Debra was determined to help me. The first time I met her, she was so energetic and happy. She said, "It's good to finally meet you. The staff at Riverwood has told me a lot about you."

"Yeah, I'm pretty messed up right now," I said with a shrug.

"I can help," she told me. Debra explained how MRS worked and the job training they did. Then she added, "It's going to take a while to get you in, but I know of another program I think will be a perfect fit."

"I'm open to anything," I said, even though I was unsure about job training. I knew how to get a job. My problem was finding a job that didn't require two good hands.

"There's a program called Jobs for Life that's part of Mosaic downtown. I think it's a good fit and you can get right in."

"All right," I said without a lot of enthusiasm. "Sign me up."

18

REUNION

Andrew

I first met Brian Bennett, the pastor of Overflow Church, in late 2008. I later learned that he spent much of our initial conversation praying, *God, don't let me say what I want to say to this guy!* In his defense, he had just read a newspaper account of what I had done, and it had made him very angry. I look back on that first meeting now and laugh because the two of us became very close friends. We corresponded weekly while I was in prison, and he also led the church to help look after my wife and daughter in my absence.

My story particularly angered Brian because he and his wife had moved to Benton Harbor less than two years before my arrest to start a church that bridged all racial and economic divides. They came not only to start a church but also to begin what was then called Overflow Christian Community Development Association, now known as Mosaic Christian Community Development Association (or Mosaic CCDA), in the heart of Benton Harbor. Brian envisioned Mosaic as a place that would impact the community through job training and creation, education, housing, and health care. The most visible parts of Mosaic are a coffee shop and café and an adjoining resale store. But it's about more than coffee and used clothes and furniture. From the start, Mosaic provided job training and entry-level jobs for people in a community with a very high unemployment rate and a significant income difference compared to its sister city, St. Joseph, the predominantly white community that's just across the St. Joseph River.

Eventually I found myself in need of one of those entry-level jobs. After leaving the discount tire store I went to work for minimum wage at a factory in nearby Coloma, Michigan, where we lived. Coloma is ten miles up I-94 from Benton Harbor. Eventually I got a small raise, but it wasn't enough to support my family.

A friend of mine told me about a job in a factory where he worked in Benton Harbor. The job started at ten dollars an hour, which may not seem like a lot, but it was quite a raise for me in 2011. Unfortunately, the work slowed down. In November 2012, the company decided it had to cut expenses, which meant laying off employees. Since I was one of the newest hires, I was one of the first let go. Moving to Colorado began to look more and more attractive.

One Sunday I mentioned losing my job to Pastor Brian. He told me Mosaic needed a part-time delivery truck driver for the resale store. Since I didn't have any other prospects, I took the job. Almost immediately the café had a part-time opening, so I took that as well. Two part-time jobs equaled one full-time job, so I stopped looking for another job. Working right in the heart of downtown Benton Harbor meant more reunions with people I had illegally put in jail, but with time, the meetings became less frequent and less heated. Occasionally I ran into someone who cussed me up one side and down the other, and I still do to this day, but I've been through so many similar encounters that I can diffuse the situation pretty quickly. I've found that when you are open and honest rather than making excuses and when you genuinely listen and offer a heartfelt apology, people respond. Proverbs 15:1 says, "A gentle answer turns away wrath, but a harsh word stirs up anger." It works every time.

I worked both jobs at Mosaic for about a year. Pastor Brian had been cor-

rect when he told me I was going to run into Jamal McGee. He still worked at
the café when I first started working there. To my great relief Jamal was not
Jameel. They might have been fraternal twins, but I never made the connection
between the two. I figured they were two people with names that sounded a lot
alike.

During my year of working the two jobs at Mosaic, the café went through
two managers. Eventually they offered me the job. This was no ordinary café
manager position. The café's primary purposes are job training and community development, not selling coffee and sandwiches. I started to feel as if I was
finally doing what I came to Benton Harbor to do back in 2003. For the first
time I felt as if I was making a difference.

A couple of years before I started at Mosaic, they had piloted a program
called Jobs for Life, an international program headquartered in North Carolina.
While Jobs for Life has made a tremendous impact on communities around the
world, it didn't go over so well at Mosaic the first time around. Out of the original ten people who signed up, only two or three actually graduated. Early in
2015 we gave it another try. But before we opened up the program to the community, the Mosaic management team, which now included me, went through
the program together. Mentoring plays a key role in the Jobs for Life program,
which is why the management team went through it first. If we were to guide
someone through the process, we needed to have already traveled that road. The
program is designed for people who have had trouble finding a job capable of
supporting their families. Believe me, I knew that journey by heart. Since my
release from prison I'd worked plenty of minimum-wage, dead-end jobs.

After the management team finished the training, people signed up for the
first class. My only connection to the program was as a mentor, and occasionally I shared my testimony to encourage people who had made mistakes.

Princella managed Jobs for Life. She and Ric, Mosaic CCDA's executive
director, did most of the actual training. They held classes across the street from
Mosaic at a place called Michigan Works! Association, which trains and con-
nects workers to area companies. During the sign-up phase before the first class

had started, I overheard Ric and Princella talking about Jamal's brother Zookie. The name didn't ring a bell for me. Nearly ten years had gone by since I'd heard it. I remember Princella saying, "I don't think Zookie will stick it out, because he doesn't look too happy to be here." Ric agreed.

One day I noticed a guy walking across the street and going into the Michigan Works! building. Someone pointed him out as Zookie. He didn't look familiar to me. Jamal came in a short time later. "Hey," I said to him, "I heard your brother's in Jobs for Life."

"Yeah," he said.

"And it's good?" I asked.

"We'll see" is all Jamal said in return.

Jameel

Riverwood didn't just introduce me to Debra Mead. They also arranged for me to receive food stamps, which enabled me to buy food. Since I still didn't have a place to store groceries or to cook, I bought mostly ready-to-eat stuff, namely, junk food. If the store had a microwave, I bought frozen food and heated it up right there. If it didn't, I bought whatever I could carry and ate it on my way.

Thanks to Dr. Carter at Riverwood, I now had more clothes than just the ones on my back. Debra also connected me with different places where I could get out of the cold and get some help when I needed it. Right after our first meeting, she even bought me a bicycle so I could get around town. I have that bike to this day. I call it my Lexus.

The biggest thing I needed was a job. The whole mess in which I found myself came down to the fact that I could no longer do the kind of physical work I'd done all my life. When some of the guys around town heard I was living on the streets, they offered to set me up in their business. This happened a lot. I always turned them down. No matter how cold or hungry I became, I was never desperate enough to sell drugs, which was the only business the guys I grew up around ever started. I don't mean that as an insult. These guys were really trying to help me. They meant well. Most of the people selling dope in poor communities like Benton Harbor do it because they don't know any different and don't have any other options. The schools are bad. Jobs don't pay a livable wage. And the drug dealers drive the best cars in town. Poor kids see this and figure it's the only way to get ahead.

I needed a job, but when Debra first took me to Jobs for Life for an interview to see if I was a good fit for the program, I resisted. I knew about Mosaic because my brother worked there for a while. The Jobs for Life program was new, which didn't matter to me. Like I said, I resisted, probably because of pride. Working had never been a problem for me. I gave everything I had to every job I ever held, even in prison. To me, this program seemed like something for people who'd never worked.

Since I didn't have any other options, I signed up. I went over to the Mosaic resale store and bought some more clothes. I figured if I was going to do this, I might as well do it right. When it came time for the classes to begin, I was there. Every day. I'd been homeless for nearly two years, and I was sick and tired of it. If this Jobs for Life program could help me get a job that was going to let me put my life back together, then I was willing to give it a try.

About three weeks into the training, the director, Princella, met with me to talk about the person she wanted to match me with. "God has just laid it on my heart that you and one of our staff members, the manager of the café, should be together. I've asked him if he will meet with you and he's agreed," she said.

"All right," I said. I still wasn't real enthusiastic about any of this, but I'd told Debra I'd do it, and I was going to keep my word. She'd done a lot to help me. I wasn't going to let her down.

"Yes," Princella said. "His name is Andrew Collins."

I nearly fell out of my chair. "Who?" I said.

"Andrew Collins," she repeated.

Homeless or not, I nearly lost it right there. All I could think was, *Nah, nah, nah! There ain't no way this is happening! No way! How can Andrew*

Collins be involved in this? Surely my brother would have told me about that.
I held it together as best I could and told her, "Miss P, I need to pray on that for a minute."

"That's fine," Princella said, completely oblivious to the fact that Andrew and I had a history together. She got up and went somewhere—I don't know where. I wasn't paying much attention to her because I was freaking out inside. I closed my eyes and said, *God, what are you doing? This can't be happening! If this is my choice, then let's do something different.* The words *my choice* stopped me right there. During my days of walking the back streets of Benton Harbor, God and I had talked a lot about the poor choices I'd made. Far too many times I did what was easy. Did I really want to do that again? Did I really want to walk away from this opportunity because I was uncomfortable?

I opened my eyes and looked down at the Jobs for Life book on my lap. I'd never really studied the cover before. The words formed a mountain. On top of the mountain I noticed two small red stickmen. I looked closely at the two men. Only then could I see that one was pulling the other up. *Wow,* I thought, *why have I never seen this before?* Now the figures jumped off the book at me. It was as if one was telling the other, "I got you. Don't worry."

God spoke to me through those two little red guys on the book. "Miss P," I said, "I think God wants me to do this. I think I *have* to do this."

"Really?" she said, surprised. "Great. Andrew's across the street at the café right now waiting for you."

"Now? Like right now?"

"Yes. I spoke with him this morning and he's ready for you."

Wow, God, you aren't giving me any space on this one, are you? "Okay. I guess I'll mosey over there," I said.

When I walked in the door of Cafe Mosaic, Andrew was seated at one of the tables. I walked over to him. He stood up and smiled and said, "Jameel McGee?"

"Uh, yeah," I said, wondering why he was asking who I was.

"Andrew Collins," he said, introducing himself. "Have a seat." I took a seat across from him. "Your brother worked here, didn't he?" Andrew asked.

"Yeah. Yeah, he did," I said, still confused.

"He's a good guy," he said. Then Andrew started explaining the program's process. The whole time he was talking, I kept thinking to myself that surely he knew who I was. I thought it was possible he didn't recognize me, because the last time we saw each other four years earlier I had long dreadlocks and was clean shaven. Now I had a beard and my head was bald. And after living on the streets for so long, I was also smaller than I had been. But still, even if he didn't recognize me, he had to know who I was by my name. I mean, he worked with my brother—my *twin* brother. We aren't identical twins, but there's no way he couldn't make the connection.

But apparently there was a way, because he didn't see it. "Let me tell you a little about myself," Andrew said. "I was a police officer here in Benton Harbor, but I did some stupid things and made some mistakes that hurt a lot of people around here. If I've wronged you or your family, please let me know so we can talk about it—"

I cut him off. "Wait a minute. You don't remember me?"

"No," he said.

I shook my head and smiled. "You serious? You really don't remember me," I said.

"How should I know you?" he asked. Now he was the one who was confused.

"Broadway Park" was all I said.

Then it clicked. "Oh shoot," he said as he pushed back his chair. "That Jameel McGee?"

"Yeah, that's me."

Andrew

The moment Jameel said the words *Broadway Park* the memory came flooding back. I could see him staring at me, squeezing the life out of my hand, jaws clenched, angry. When he walked away that day I thought I'd never get a chance to make things right with him.

"I am so sorry, man," I said. As I said this I remembered how angry he was the last time we saw each other. I did a quick look around the café and back toward the resale store to see how many customers we had, just in case I had to do some damage control. I had no idea what might be about to happen.

"It's fine," Jameel said with a look and a tone that made me think it really might be fine.

"No, it's not fine," I said. "I hurt you and I am so sorry for that, for everything I did to you."

"It's taken care of. It's over. It's done. It's forgiven," Jameel said.

We went back and forth like this for what seemed like a very long time. Finally, Jameel stopped me and said, "It's taken care of because God's got it. I don't deal with that situation because I gave it over to God. It's his now. I have nothing to do with it."

"There's got to be something more I can do," I said.

"Man, if you want to do something more, then you gotta take that up with God," he said. "Right now, I'm just trying to get my life back together." Jameel went on to tell me about all he'd been through over the past couple of years and all the roadblocks he still faced. "I'm just tired from dealing with it all," he said. "I'm worn out. If it keeps going like it has been going, my next step is just to say 'Bye, everybody' and be done with it."

I saw the hurt in Jameel's eyes. "That's heavy," I said. "You seem tired." When I said those words, he began to tear up and look away. I've been there before, betrayed by my own emotions. It was clear Jameel no longer wanted to fake it and wear a happy mask. I didn't know what else to say, so I said, "Can we pray?"

"Yeah, let's pray," Jameel said.

So I started praying. I began by praying for Jameel and what he was going through. Then I thanked God for what had just happened and asked him to bless what was to come. I asked him to bless this opportunity to grow together and to bless our friendship, which probably sounded really odd because, honestly, how do you become friends with someone who lied and put you in federal prison and generally ruined your life? But I prayed it anyway.

After I said amen, I looked over at Jameel. "You think we can do this?" I asked.

Jameel smiled and nodded. "I think God wants us to do it."

"There's a lot of history between us," I cautioned. "Do you really think we can move beyond it all and go forward?"

"Yeah, we gotta be able to do that. And if we can move forward, then maybe we can teach other people how to do the same," he said.

"Okay," I said, relieved. "We'll meet on Tuesday, then."

"Tuesday it is," Jameel said.

After Jameel left, I went into the back room of the café. I walked past one of the girls who worked for me and then burst into tears. She came over and put her arm on my back. "Drew, what's wrong? What's wrong?"

"I . . ." I had trouble forcing the words out. "I put that dude in prison with a ten-year sentence."

"What!?" she said. "What did he say to you?" The way she said it made me think she thought Jameel had laid into me.

I looked over at her. "He forgave me."

As soon as I said that, I lost it completely. The dam of emotions broke. I felt like I did the day I first confessed everything to my pastor and to God. A lightness came over me. I felt clean. I felt . . . forgiven.

Later that day the girl told me she was moving to Indianapolis. That meant I had a job opening I needed to fill.

19

BEYOND FORGIVENESS

Andrew

I had never heard Jameel's side of the story of his arrest until maybe the second or third time we met as part of the Jobs for Life program. It wasn't because he'd never told me. He told me his side of the story when I first confronted him at the door of the convenience store on Fair Street in February 2006. But at that moment I wasn't interested in what he had to say. I already knew everything I needed to know. Of course he claimed he didn't know anything about the dope in the car. Of course he swore it wasn't his and he didn't have anything to do with it.

In all my time on the police department, no one I busted ever said, "Okay, you got me. I'm guilty." Even if I caught someone with dope in their jeans pocket, they'd claim they put on their brother's pants that morning and had no idea how that dope got there. I expected Jameel, who I thought was Ox at the time, to say he didn't have anything to do with the crack I knew was his. Everyone I ever arrested said that, including the guy I arrested with Jameel that morning.

When I arrested Jameel, I knew he was exactly the guy

I was looking for. That's why I lied on the police report and in my testimony at his trial. I knew—I mean I *absolutely* knew—that was his dope, and I was not going to let him get off on what I saw as a technicality.

After we met at Mosaic, I wasn't so sure. Nearly every person the feds set free after my confession had ended up back in prison. Jameel didn't. That gave me serious doubts about him being the big-time dealer I was after. But at the very least, I thought he had to have been an accomplice to the other guy in the car. If the dope in the cup holder had not been Jameel's, he at least knew what was going down with the drug deal I'd set up through my informant. He and the other guy had to be working together.

Even after meeting with him and apologizing for how I had hurt him—and I had hurt him terribly because my lies had put him in prison—part of me deep down inside did not want to believe he was completely innocent. This belief had nothing to do with Jameel. It had everything to do with me. Even after all these years since I'd been caught and confessed and came clean with God, the city of Benton Harbor, the United States of America, and my victims, I could not bring myself to admit I had put an innocent man in prison. I still held on to a thin shred of hope that despite all the wrong I'd done, I had not sunk to that level of depravity. People were hurt, but it's not like they were fine, upstanding pillars of the community. I could even justify taking the money that belonged to dealers. It wasn't as though they'd earned that money through hard work. I'm not trying to minimize what I did. All I'm saying is I wanted to hold on to a last shred of dignity as a police officer. I tried to believe that deep down my motives had been pure, that all I really wanted to do was get bad people off the streets.

And then I made the mistake of asking Jameel about the day of his arrest. I asked because even though I did not want him to be innocent, I had to know one way or the other. This wasn't the first time I'd asked someone a question like this. I did it pretty much every time I was reunited with a person I had put away. Obviously, I didn't bring up the arrest if the person appeared ready to hurt me. And I always apologized for what I had done before I brought up anything else. Asking these kinds of questions in no way trivialized what I had done. This was just about easing my own conscience.

I don't remember exactly how I brought the arrest up with Jameel. I didn't do it in the middle of a heavy conversation. Instead, I waited for a light moment and then said something like, "You know, on the day I arrested you, I never could find the car keys on you. Where'd you hide them?"

"I never had the keys," Jameel responded. "I never drove that car."

"Really?" I asked. Inside I felt my last little wall of self-defense about to crumble.

"No, man. That wasn't my car. I was the passenger. I needed to get to the store to buy my baby some milk before he got to my house. I needed a ride, so I asked Will. Next thing I know, I'm getting arrested," he said. "If you'd checked out the security tape from the store, you would have seen that."

"So you had nothing to do with the drugs in the car?" I asked.

"Nope. I didn't know anything about what Will was up to. I didn't even know his real name. He was at my grandmother's house with one of my cousins when I needed a ride. When we got to the store, I loaned him my phone. That's all."

And that's when it hit me. I actually heard what he was saying, not as a cop with his mind already made up, but as a person sitting across from an innocent man in Cafe Mosaic on a very ordinary weekday morning. "So you were completely innocent," I said.

"Yep," Jameel said.

"Oh man," I said, broken. "I am so sorry I did that to you."

"I told you, Drew, I gave all that over to God. We're good. It's all forgiven," he said.

"No, no, no. There's got to be something more I can do for you," I said.

"No man. There's nothing."

"Don't you want to punch me or something?" I asked, only half joking.

Honestly, I think I'd have felt better if he had punched me. At the time I had no idea that while he was in prison, he fantasized about beating me to death. I didn't know any of that until we started writing this book together. If I'd known, I probably wouldn't have said it. But in that moment I felt I had to do something more than apologize. Saying I was sorry felt so small in comparison to how much damage I'd done to his life.

"No," Jameel said with a big smile. "I don't want to punch you. Like I told you, bro, if you want to do something more, take it up with God. I gave it to him. This is his deal now."

I held it together for the rest of our meeting time. We moved on in the conversation to whatever it was we were supposed to talk about that day for the Jobs for Life program. But after he left I went off by myself and thought about what had just transpired. A whole new level of guilt and shame and regret rose up in me. My mind could hardly process the truth that now dawned on me. I did not break down and weep as I had after our first meeting. Those tears came out of the joy of being forgiven. Now I was trying to understand how much Jameel had actually forgiven. All I could think of was how I had destroyed his life. Not only had I put him in prison, but I had kept him from seeing his son for the first time.

And he has forgiven me . . . kept running through my head.

Later that evening I called my mom and told her, "I think I put an innocent man in prison." She listened while I talked through everything I was feeling. I told her how I knew I'd hurt people but I always thought my crime had been in going too far. "I never thought anyone I put away was actually"—I could hardly say the word—"innocent. But he was. I really put an innocent man in prison."

My mom listened, which she is really good at.

Since that conversation I've come to realize just how much I took away from Jameel. After surveying the totality of what was taken, I've come to the conclusion that the most harmful thing I did to him was take his voice away. As he cried out from jail those first couple of days, telling people he was not the person I was looking for, I took his voice away. When he relayed all the lies and deceit in my report to his lawyer and then heard each argument destroyed by more lies, I took his voice away. After every denied appeal, his voice was taken away.

To this day, the part of his story that haunts me the most is the fact that his own family, his own flesh and blood, believed he was the drug kingpin I had made him out to be. Voiceless. How many more voices have I stolen? Whose voices am I stifling now? My relationship with Jameel will forever change the way I evaluate all my relationships. I pray this book gives him his voice back.

The next time I saw Jameel, I apologized again. And again. I still do it to this day. Every time, he just smiles at me and tells me, "Drew, bro, we're good. Quit apologizing."

Maybe someday I will be able to stop. I haven't reached that point yet.

20

A FRIENDSHIP EMERGES

Jameel

I don't really know why I opened up to Andrew during that first meeting at Mosaic. Before I walked into the café, I had no idea how the conversation might go, but I never imagined it might include spilling my guts. I am a very private person. When things aren't going too good, I shut down. No one except Dr. Carter at Riverwood knew how low my life had become. And yet there I was with the last person on earth I wanted to see, much less talk to, confessing I was tired and worn out and not too far from just checking out once and for all. God had to be the one to open my mouth. I don't have any other explanation.

God's timing did play a big part. Right before I met with Drew that morning, the Jobs for Life class talked about the pit. The speaker discussed how all the roadblocks in your life history have put you where you are. Life throws some of these roadblocks at you, and others you make yourself. After banging up against these roadblocks over and over again, you find yourself in an emotional pit where all you can do is focus on yourself. The pit gets so deep you can't see the people who want to help you. You just look down, stuck, unable to crawl out. If by chance you manage to scratch your way up toward the top of the pit, the other people down there with you pull you back in.

Everything in this lesson spoke to me. Everything. I thought more and more about the pit I found myself in. My homelessness didn't dig my pit, and neither did hurting my hand, which made it hard for me to work. Those are the obstacles. I'd dug my pit when I cut everyone else off and shut down emotionally. I sat at the bottom of my pit, focusing only on myself, and I couldn't see the hands offering to pull me up. I think that's why the book cover illustration of the one guy pulling up the other guy jumped out at me. God used it to tell me it was time for me to reach up and take someone's hand.

Maybe that's why I opened up and told Drew how much I was hurting. I needed to reach up and take someone's hand, and his was the closest. Now that I think about it, he had to be the one. Who better to share my burden with than the one I had forgiven for the part he had in creating the obstacles that eventually led to my pit? It was as though by forgiving Drew, I stopped blaming him for where I was. And that set me free to let him help me out.

Andrew

The timing of Jameel's coming in right when one of our employees had turned in her notice to quit had to be more than coincidence. I saw it as divine timing. Even so, I was a little nervous about asking him to work at Cafe Mosaic. Working as someone's boss can put a strain on even a good relationship. I didn't know what our relationship might be yet, but *good* wasn't the word I'd use to describe it. Yet the more I thought and prayed about it, the more convinced I became that I should offer him the job.

The next time Jameel came in for our scheduled meeting, I bluntly asked him, "Are you a good employee? We've had an awkward enough relationship as it is." Jameel didn't know it yet, but I wanted to offer him a job.

"What?" Jameel asked.

"One of the women who works for me just turned in her two-weeks notice. I need to hire someone to replace her. It's just a part-time job, but it's a start," I said.

Jameel looked at me with that big smile of his. "Are you serious?" he asked.

"Yeah, I am. How would you like to work for Cafe Mosaic?"

As soon as I asked him if he wanted the job, I saw a Jameel I had never seen before. He lit up. "Yeah. Yeah, I think I would. Now, I have an issue with my hand, but I think I'll be able to handle it," he said.

I didn't know about a hand issue, but I didn't think this was the time to ask more about it. Instead, I asked, "Do you want to jump behind the counter and try it out and see if it works for you?"

"Let's do it," he said.

I showed him how to steam milk and make some of the coffee drinks. Two weeks later he officially started. From the start I realized asking him if he was a good employee was a ridiculous question. The man has an unbelievable work ethic. He not only went above and beyond whatever I asked of him but also constantly looked for ways to do his job better. Because the café is an entry-level job, and part time at that, no one works there for long. At first Jameel worked fewer than ten hours a week. Before long other people left, and I was able to increase his hours until he got up to around thirty or thirty-five hours a week.

With the two of us working closely together, I quickly figured out Jameel was homeless. The weather turns cold early in Michigan, which made me start bombarding him with questions about where he was going to stay and what he needed before winter came. I even tried to arrange things where he could come stay in my basement. I approached Krissy about it one night, and she gave me a very curious look before asking if I was serious. She said, "I'm glad you two are getting along, but what if he were to snap one night and kill you in your sleep?"

Jameel and I hadn't known each other long. The thought of waking up with him standing at my bedside was a chilling thought. Maybe there were other options.

When we first started working together, I don't think either of us thought we might become friends. However, the space behind the counter is pretty small, which meant we worked in close proximity. Before we started working together, our conversations had all been about my putting him in prison or the Jobs for Life material. Back behind the counter we started talking about everything. Even though we are very different, the two of us found we have a lot in common. We just sort of clicked. Without realizing it or giving it a lot of thought, the two of us became friends.

Since we are both dads, we talked a lot about the challenges of being a father. Jameel talked to me about how little time he got to spend with his son. Once again I apologized because if it wasn't for me, he might be closer to him. And once again Jameel told me to stop apologizing. Since his ex had moved out of state, he assured me his time with his son would have been limited even if I had never entered his life.

Jameel might not have been able to spend much time with his son, but he was very proud of him. His son played football and now lived in Fort Wayne, Indiana. One day at work he started talking about a football awards banquet coming up the next day. Fort Wayne is two and a half hours from Benton Harbor by car, but Jameel didn't have a car. I couldn't drive him because I had a speaking engagement that night, but I really wanted to find a way for him to go. I texted my men's group and told them what was going on and asked if anyone could drive him to the banquet. One of my friends said he would be happy to do it. And then a snowstorm started to roll through. My friend still drove Jameel to Fort Wayne.

One day during a slow time, I overheard Jameel talking on the phone. Then the call started getting heated. Normally Jameel is one of the most chill guys I know. Nothing gets under his skin. He joked and laughed with workers and customers and never stopped smiling. On this day, however, the phone conversation brought back the Jameel I'd met in Broadway Park. He was as angry as I had ever seen him. When the call ended he kept shaking his head and was trembling all over, as if he were about to explode.

"What's going on?" I asked. "What's wrong?"

He tried to talk but couldn't. He stood there, shaking with anger.

I dove right in. "Look, whatever it is, bro, it's not worth making a stupid decision and ending up back in jail or anything like that. Let's talk about it. What's going on?"

Slowly, he calmed down enough to where he could talk. He explained the situation, which involved his son. I listened closely before I said a word. Finally I said, "Your ex is playing games with you, trying to get you stirred up. Every time you respond, it just fuels that fire. Let it die down. Stop responding and eventually it will blow itself out." I talked about my own relationships and how I'd seen this work in them.

Jameel pulled himself together and made it through the rest of the day. The next morning when he came in, I saw a different Jameel. He came straight over to me and gave me a big hug. "Bro, thank you, man. You were right. I went home last night and took time to process everything. I took your advice and it worked. Thank you."

Jameel

After I started the Jobs for Life program, I stayed in touch with Debra Mead. She knew I had a passion for music, so she told me about a church that had a strong band and all kinds of musical equipment, a church called Overflow. I knew about Overflow because Mosaic was part of it and Andrew had already invited me to go there with him. Every time he asked I told him the same thing: "I don't really do the church thing."

Debra also knew I didn't do the church thing, but that didn't stop her from talking to me about it. One day we were talking and the conversation turned to music. That led to her talking about Overflow church again. "I know you have a lot of church hurt in your past and you don't want to deal with that, but you could go over during their band practice and just check it out instead of going on a Sunday," she said.

I was hesitant but eventually I agreed to go.

The next Thursday evening I rode my bike over to the building where the church met. I did a double take at the sign to make sure I was in the right place. This didn't look like any church building I'd ever seen. I'd actually ridden past the building many times. For years I wondered what it was. Now I knew it was a church that looked nothing like a church. There was no brick. No steeple. No stained-glass windows. None of that. The nonchurchy appearance made me feel better about going inside.

I made my way to the auditorium, which didn't look like any church sanctuary I'd seen before. Debra had told band members about me and how I had experience working with the mixer board. One of the guys in charge invited me to go upstairs to their sound room. They were shorthanded and needed my help. The band started playing and I had to admit they were pretty good. I mean, this was not some church group with a piano and organ. This was a real band like the ones I'd worked with in Milan and Terre Haute.

During a break one of the drummers introduced himself. The two of us started talking, and he told me a little of his story and how he had ended up at Overflow. When he asked about me, I told him part of my story, including my passion for music. I did not tell him I was homeless. I kept that to myself.

After we talked for a while, the drummer asked, "Are you going to come back and check us out on Sunday?"

"Yeah, I will," I lied. I returned the following night for band practice—they practiced both Thursday and Friday nights—but I didn't go to the service on Sunday. I also didn't make it back for band practice the next week.

That might have been the end of it, but I woke up early the next Sunday with God telling me to ride my bike to Overflow. I was like, *Okay, I'll give it a try and check it out, but I'm not making any promises to do anything beyond that.*

I rode my bike over and arrived in time for the nine o'clock service. I found a seat over on one side and just took it all in. The first thing I noticed was the church's racial dynamic. A lot of the churches I'd seen were all black or all white. This was one of the first I'd seen outside of prison that was mixed. The way people dressed was also very different from the churches my mother took me to when I was a kid. No one was dressed to impress. Everyone appeared pretty laid back.

All right, I thought, *that's cool. I like this.*

The band started playing and I got into the music. I knew what to expect from having sat in on their practice session. Then the preacher got up to speak. I couldn't help but listen. It was like he knew everything I'd been battling in my brain. He must have been able to read my mind, because he talked about letting God be in control and how when we are in control, we make a mess of things. That might make some people mad, but this was exactly what I needed to hear.

When the service ended, I told God, *This is a nice church. I'm glad I came. I think I can come back.* That's when I noticed the next service started in two minutes. I didn't realize they had an early and a late service. I sat down and stayed put. The band played the same songs, the preacher preached the same message, but I didn't mind. I needed to hear that sermon twice. Both times I got something different out of it.

When the second service ended, people hung around, talking and hugging and just chilling. Several came over and talked to me. This place had a really loving atmosphere that I knew I needed. I told God right then, *This is going to be my church.* Nobody judged me there. No one cared who you had been or what you had done. They were just real. I needed to be a part of this.

This was a really big step for me, more than just deciding to attend a church. During the time I'd been homeless and in my Jobs for Life classes, I had spent a lot of time examining how I ended up where I was. Everything always came back to the same place: I had to let it go, not just the anger I once had for Andrew, but everything. I had to let go of control over my own life and surrender it to Jesus. I'd wrestled with him long enough. At just the right times he'd come into my life to rescue me from some of the situations I'd put myself in, but he wanted more than that from me. He wanted everything. I finally told him okay. I let it all go to him. I made a statement at church saying I had done this and then followed it up by being baptized. This church that didn't look like a church didn't have a real baptistery. Instead, they brought in a horse trough and filled it full of water. Andrew helped baptize me in November 2015.

I haven't been the same since.

I hadn't worked at Cafe Mosaic very long before people recognized Drew and me. The questions started right off. "How can you do it?" a lot of people asked.

"Do what?" I always replied.

"How can you work here?"

"How can you work with him?"

"How can you be around him every day?"

"How can the two of you be friends?"

Really, everything came down to one question: "How could you forgive him?"

The question goes beyond what you might think. To understand why people had such a hard time believing I could actually forgive Drew, you have to understand the culture in which I grew up. On just a human level, people have trouble with forgiveness, but on the streets where I grew up, it's even tougher. Every day you not only have to look out for yourself but you also better be strong or people are going to run right over you. Being strong means you avenge any wrong done to you. If someone hits you or pushes you, you have to push back harder. You don't just let things go, because if you do, people won't stop pushing and taking until there's nothing left of you.

When I battled God in Broadway Park, this was what I was fighting against. So when people asked how I could forgive Drew, it wasn't just that they couldn't understand how I could turn loose of the hurt. They didn't understand how I could give up my payback, much less become friends with this guy.

I've had a lot of conversations with people, and I always tell them the same thing: You've got to get God in there. In life, everything is not to be avenged. That's not ours to do anyway. Romans 12:19–21 says,

Do not take revenge, my friends, but leave room for God's wrath, for it is written: "It is mine to avenge; I will repay," says the Lord. On the contrary:

"If your enemy is hungry, feed him;
　　if he is thirsty, give him something to drink.
In doing this, you will heap burning coals on his head."

Do not be overcome by evil, but overcome evil with good.

I told everyone who asked that I had to give everything over to God. I could not forgive Drew on my own, but God could do it. Some people looked at me as if these were just words. When I saw that look, I went even further. I told them to take a look at my life and the mess I made when I was in control and notice how change came when I surrendered to God's control. I had these conversations while I still didn't have a house of my own and after I moved into the house in which I now live. I wasn't talking about a change in my circumstances but a change in me. I stopped being the angry, hurt, keep-to-himself man people had seen walking the back streets of Benton Harbor. When they see me now, they see a different me.

I'm free. But I didn't do it. God did.

Some people got it. Others didn't. That didn't matter to me. I kept telling them anyway.

21

IT IS WELL

Andrew

One day in November 2015, Princella's husband, Jim, a UPS driver and one of the tech guys at our church, stopped in the café. He came into the café a lot, so I didn't think anything of it. Often he brought lunch for Princella. Cafe Mosaic serves some great food, but you can only eat there so many days in a row before you want something else. When I saw Jim walk in, I thought this was probably nothing more than another lunch run for his wife. Even when he came over to the counter, I thought he was just being polite and saying hello.

"Andrew, Jameel," he called to both of us, "I have something I need the two of you to think about." Jameel was close by.

"What's up?" I asked.

"Pastor Brian and I have been talking about the two of you and your story, and we wondered if you might be willing to do a video," Jim said.

Jameel and I sort of looked at each other. We'd been working together less than two months at this point. "What do you think, bro?" I asked.

"Geez, I don't know. Yeah, I guess I'd be okay with that," he said.

"Yeah, I think that will be all right," I said. This was the first time we'd been asked to do anything like this.

"All right. I'll let Pastor Brian know. We'll set something up soon," Jim said.

A week or so later Jameel and I were back at the convenience store on Fair Street for the first time since the arrest. Jim and Jameel went into the store to film parts that set up Jameel's walking out and being accosted by me. I sat outside, waiting. Fair Street isn't exactly one of my favorite places to hang out. Back when I was a cop, I used to do a lot of business in the neighborhoods near the store. At that time, there were some blocks nearby where you could throw a rock in any direction and hit a drug house or witness a drug deal going down at almost any time, day or night.

I'd been outside waiting for maybe five minutes when a guy came walking straight for me. I recognized him right off. Several years earlier he had taken off running when I tried to arrest him. The foot chase ended when I got close enough to fire my Taser and bring him down. I remembered it very clearly and so did he.

The guy got in my face and started cussing at me. He yelled and screamed and called me every name he could think of while asking me what I was doing back in this neighborhood. Proverbs 15:1 kept running through my head: "A gentle answer turns away wrath, but a harsh word stirs up anger." This guy's anger was pretty stirred up already, so I didn't want to say anything to make the situation worse.

When the angry man realized he wasn't getting anywhere with me, he stormed into the store, grumbling and cursing the whole way. Because of the filming, I knew I'd still be here when he came out. I hoped he'd calm down before he returned.

A few minutes later the man came out of the store, but the look on his face was completely different. Instead of anger, I now saw fear. Then I saw Jameel. He had the guy by the back of his neck and was basically pushing him along. I saw he was talking right into the guy's ear. *Whoa. What's this?* I thought. Once Jameel had the guy clear of the store door, his grip on the guy's neck only seemed to get firmer. That's when I realized where Jameel was taking him. The two were coming straight to me.

Jameel

Jim wanted to start filming inside the store as a way of setting up my walking outside and having Andrew get up in my face. He wanted to recreate that scene, which was cool with me. I only hoped I could keep a straight face while we were doing it. Being back in the store did not stir up old feelings. When I say that was all in the past, I mean it really is in the past.

I was inside the store talking to Jim when this guy I knew from the neighborhood burst through the door yelling. It took me a moment to catch what he was saying between all the cursing and yelling. The guy saw me and directed his shouting my way, as if I wanted to hear what he had to say. "Did you know that no-good Collins is right outside?" Then he went off on all he wanted to do to Drew because Drew had tased him and arrested him and all of that.

"Hey, man, just chill," I said. "You don't need to come into a place of business yelling like that."

He didn't stop. He kept going on and on about that no-good Collins, only he used a lot of adjectives we've tried to avoid using in this book.

"Look, dude, cool it," I said, trying to remain calm and settle him down. "The guy ain't a cop anymore, and he went to prison for the things he did. Leave it at that. There's no need for you to carry on now just because you saw him outside."

"Whadaya talking about? Do you know what he did to me?" the guy yelled at me.

And that's when he pushed me too far.

"Hey!" I yelled and then told him in terms he might understand that he needed to shut his mouth *now*! I got right up in his face and laid into him with truth. "So you're all mad and upset about this cop who treated you rough, and you think you got cause to be angry? Dude, I know you. I know what you did. You were guilty. He caught you red handed. Everybody knows you were selling dope back then and you still do today. You ain't got nothing to hold on to or to be mad about. You're just mad because he caught you doing what you know you shouldn't have been doing in the first place. You know what I'm saying?"

I didn't wait for him to respond.

"Yeah, man, you mad 'cause you got caught when you were guilty! I was innocent and I went to prison, but I've let it go. So what's your problem? I don't care if he caught you or not. If you were caught doing something illegal, that's on you. You know what I'm saying? That's your problem, not his. Own up to it. Be a man. I'm telling you, if that was my dope and I'd been caught, I'd have owned up to it. I'm not letting anyone go down because of my mess. I'd accept the consequences. So should you. You need to stop being stupid and stop doing stupid stuff."

"I . . . uh . . . ," the guy mumbled at me.

I wasn't finished. "So you come into this store talking and screaming where everyone can hear. If you think you really have a legitimate gripe with Collins, you need to talk to him. All this yapping about what you're going to do is irrelevant. The man is right outside. You got a problem with him, you go talk to him."

The guy looked at me like he was in shock. I knew what he was thinking. "Yeah, you thought you could come in here like you were fixing to get me to be the cosigner on what you've messed up. That's not happening." I paused for a moment, then grabbed him by the back of the neck. "You know what? You got a problem with Collins, well, we're going to settle it right now."

I then proceeded to push him out of the store and right toward Drew. I kept talking to him the whole way out. When we got over to Drew, the guy's tune had completely changed. I pushed the guy forward a little and said, "You got something to say, now's the time. Otherwise, you keep your mouth shut." I released my hold on his neck and stood back.

The guy looked at me and then turned back to Andrew. He dropped his head and said, "I'm sorry I yelled at you."

The look on Andrew's face as he looked at me was one of relief.

"That's okay, man. I'm sorry I was so rough with you all those years ago. You know, I'm a new person today. In fact, that's why Zookie and I are out here. We're making a video about forgiveness to show at our church, Overflow."

"Yeah, brother, why don't you come over to our church and check it out," I said.

The guy mumbled something, then got out of there as fast as he could. We never did see him in church. I believe he's in prison today for selling drugs.

After the guy left, Andrew looked at me and said, "Wow. I know you've got me now."

"Ain't nothing to it," I said. "You know I got your back."

We then tried to shoot the video, but between the cars on the streets and the wind and people going in and out of the store, it just didn't work. We ended up shooting the whole thing in someone's basement. Instead of recreating the scene of the arrest, we just talked about it. We did have some video from inside the store when the guy came in yelling, but we couldn't use that in church.

Andrew

The Sunday Pastor Brian planned to show the video turned out to be a rough morning for me. I came into church with a huge weight on my shoulders that had absolutely nothing to do with Jameel. There are some hurts that just don't seem to go away, and I felt one on this particular Sunday. Someone who had hurt me in the past, someone close to me, had hurt me again in spite of endless promises that this time things would be different. Things weren't different. I made myself vulnerable and got burned in the process.

The eleven o'clock service started with the band playing the old song "It Is Well with My Soul." I could not sing along because it was not well with my soul. Our church is a very open place. When people have things they're dealing with, there's a freedom for them to kneel at the front and do business with God. Usually this takes place at the end of the service, but not always. As I tried to sing along with the congregation, I felt God pushing me to go up and pray. I couldn't change the person who'd hurt me, but I could change the way I responded, because the way I had responded so far was not good. The song kept going and God kept pushing, but I pushed back. *They're showing the video this morning. If I go up, people will think I'm just drawing attention to myself,* I argued with God.

The song ended. As soon as it did I knew I'd missed my moment.

The service continued. The band played a few more songs before Pastor Brian delivered his message about racial reconciliation. Overflow is a great place for such a message because every imaginable demographic—age, race, income bracket—worships there. I did my best to listen, but I wasn't thinking about racial reconciliation and forgiveness. I couldn't because I had someone close to me whom I was struggling to forgive. I didn't want to. This person had hurt me so much and I wanted to hurt them back.

Then the video started. I felt like the world's biggest hypocrite as I watched it. Up on the screen Jameel was talking about forgiving me, and yet I couldn't bring myself to forgive this person in my life. I'd said I'd forgiven them, but I could not accept them for who they are and move past the hurt. At the same time, I noticed people looking at me in surprise.

Nearly ten years had passed since I'd arrested Jameel and six had passed since I went to prison. In that time a lot of new people had moved into the area and become a part of the church. Those staring at me had no idea I'd been a cop who went to prison. That wasn't exactly something I advertised. "Hi, I'm Andrew and I used to be a bad cop" was not the way I introduced myself. Now everyone knew, which I was fine with. I really was. I wanted them to know, yet that only made me feel even more like a hypocrite. *Jameel forgave me. We're close now. Why can't I forgive?*

The video ended. The pastor said a few words about how powerful the message was. He invited anyone who needed to do business with God about forgiveness and reconciliation to take the time to do that before they left. Then the band got up to play a final song. Wouldn't you know it? As if on cue, they played "It Is Well with My Soul" again. I'd missed my first chance. I wasn't going to miss this one. I went up to the altar, got down on my knees, and started praying. In the back of my mind, I knew everyone probably assumed I was there because of what had happened between Jameel and me. That kept me from coming forward earlier in the service. It was not going to this time. I knelt down and prayed and asked God to give me the grace to turn loose of the hurt and pain once and for all.

I'd been at the front for a while when I felt an arm around me. Then I heard a voice praying over me. It was Jameel.

Jameel

This was just a regular Sunday for me. I loved being there and I loved using my gifts and passions in the tech booth. I mixed the sound for the band and basically just enjoyed myself. When the pastor started his message, I knew this was going to be good. He was on point that day. I was excited.

I had not yet seen the finished video. I could have but I chose not to. It took a while to edit it down. Pastor Brian wanted a five-minute video. Jim—the man who shot the video—struggled to edit the footage down to eleven or twelve minutes.

As the video played, I listened to the crowd. I heard people ooh and aah and react emotionally to what was being said on screen. That was good. But I was afraid they'd get only the negative part of the story. I did not want them to come away thinking that all these horrible things had been done to me and that life was so unfair. Yes, I'd gone through bad stuff, but God had already made this all good. I didn't even think about the bad anymore. Those times are so far behind me today that it's unbelievable. Everything I went through God used to make me into the man I am today. I don't carry any anger or regrets over it, and I didn't want anyone to start carrying them for me.

When the band started playing the final song, I noticed Drew go up and kneel down to pray. *Oh man, I hope he's not dealing with the oohs and aahs from the crowd when they showed the video.* I made some adjustments on the mixer board and then looked back at Drew. *Do I go down there?* I wondered. Then I thought about the fear I had with the video, that people might come away focused on the bad and not the good. That settled it. I told the other guys in the booth, "I'll be right back," then started toward Drew. To get from the control booth to the front of the church meant going down a couple of long hallways and then down a flight of stairs. I didn't know if he'd still be praying when I finally got there. If he wasn't, I'd just wait for the service to end, then start disconnecting equipment like I did every Sunday.

Everyone in the church who was looking up could see me as I walked from the side entrance of the auditorium over to Drew, which made me hesitate for a moment. I wished we could do this in private. I knelt down next to him, put my arm around him, and started praying. I didn't know what he was dealing with, but I didn't need to. Something was weighing heavy on him, so I prayed something like, "God, whether this is guilt over what happened between Drew and me or something else, let him know that you have already taken care of this. You've got it. Help him trust you and let it go." I said amen and started to stand up. Drew stayed on his knees. He looked up at me as if he were going to say something, but he didn't.

I patted him on the shoulder and said, "I love you, man." Then I stood up to go back to the control room. The service was ending and I had work to do. I looked back at Drew, and he just lost it, crying. That's when I knew I really needed to get back to the control room. If I stayed there with him, I'd lose it too.

The music stopped playing. I started unplugging cameras, then went upstairs to turn everything off in the control room. When I came back downstairs, Drew was still up front, still praying and weeping. An older couple stopped me and talked to me for a few minutes. I didn't stick around for long. As soon as I could, I got out of the conversation, jumped on my bike, and pedaled home. It had been an awesome day, but I was ready to get home.

Andrew

When Jameel first came down and started praying, part of me was like, *Okay, buddy, say amen so I can get back to what I'm dealing with.* When he finally did say amen, I turned to say thank you because in spite of my annoyance, his praying for me really was a nice gesture.

And then Jameel said, "I love you, man."

I put my head down and could not say another word. I began bawling from the weight of the fact that I couldn't forgive a person who had not done one-tenth of what I'd done to Jameel. And here was Jameel, offering up his love to me like a true brother. In that moment Jameel was truly a flesh-and-blood version of Jesus to me because he'd forgiven me of so much without asking for anything in return.

"*I love you, man.*" I didn't deserve that love. I didn't deserve his forgiveness or his friendship or his love. How, then, could I hold back and not forgive the one who had hurt me? Everything just poured out of me. Other leaders in the church came and prayed over me. By the time I finally got up, the church was empty. Everyone had gone except for a few stragglers. Pastor Brian asked me if I was okay.

I smiled. "Yeah. I am. I really am."

EPILOGUE

In February 2016 Jameel moved into a house of his own in Benton Harbor. A few days after moving in, he convinced the local drug dealers to leave his street once and for all. Neighbors who had lived on the block for decades finally had their neighborhood back. Later that summer he started an afternoon mentoring program for children in the area. He named it Jameel's Ultimate Mentoring Program, or JUMP. The program includes music, which Jameel teaches using the studio he's built in his new home. He also parked his bike and bought a car.

Andrew left Cafe Mosaic in the summer of 2016 to join the area staff of Young Life. He now works with local schools to reach at-risk kids, giving them hope for a better future.

Jameel left Cafe Mosaic a few weeks later, taking a job with Emergency Shelter Services (ESS), a nonprofit that provides temporary housing for families and single parents with children and assists them in finding permanent homes. He spends his days helping homeless adults and families find a home of their own. ESS helped Jameel get into his home, and now he returns the favor for others.

Even though they no longer work together at Mosaic, Jameel and Andrew still spend a great deal of time together. They now tell their story to organizations across the country. On one of those trips, Jameel spent Father's Day with his son for the first time.

When they aren't traveling together, Jameel and Andrew often just hang out or take their children out together. They don't just have a great story. They truly are best friends.

ACKNOWLEDGMENTS

Bruce Nygren and the hardworking team at Penguin Random House. We can't imagine we'll ever understand all that went into telling our story. Thank you for what you do.

Wes Yoder. Thank you for your expertise as a literary agent. You are an incredible example of the power of love. We meet people all over the country from all walks of life who know Wes Yoder. Yet we've never heard one negative word. You live a life of love! We're still waiting for our time on your front porch sipping sweet tea.

Mark Tabb. You are a master storyteller. Thank you for your heart for Jesus and your passion for justice. Jesus handpicked you to write this book. Watching you (digitally) write this book in three weeks was amazing. Looking forward to reading the rest of your books.

From Andrew

Jeff and Lakita Wright. You both do so much for the kingdom. Amid marriage ministry, a thriving urban ministry, and the numerous boards you are on, you had time to take a call from me as I sat overwhelmed with what God was doing in this story. Without you I wouldn't know Wes.

Pastor Brian Rumor of New Life Church. My life forever changed when you showed me grace and challenged me in my faith.

Pastor Brian Bennett of Overflow Church. Your drive is astounding; your love for people and justice is infectious. Your loyalty and friendship are cherished. Thank you for joining our family on this roller coaster.

The Tuesday Morning Men's Group, both present and past members. I am the man I am today because God continues to use your wisdom and guidance to mold me.

Mom and Ike. I am strong because of you. Compassionate because of you.

Driven because of you. I can't think of two other people I've shed so many tears with. Thank you for your unconditional love.

Mark and Chuck. I am a better father because of the two of you.

Grandma and Grandpa. I know Jesus because of you. You've modeled his love and grace my entire life. I'll enjoy joining you, sipping coffee, and eating Little Debbie's for eternity. You introduced me to my Savior and helped me grow deeper in my faith.

Kyle and Ditte. I stay driven because you stay driven. I can't wait to read your book of true love. You inspire more people than you know.

Kiya. Sweet Kiya. It might be weird for a father to say he looks up to his daughter, but I do. What a joy to watch you grow and mature. I think each phase is my favorite, but a new attribute in your personality comes as you grow older, leaving me thinking that now is my favorite season. Thank you for joining me in my adventures. Please allow me to have picnics with you until I'm an old man! They mean the world to me.

Krissy. When we said "I do," we didn't realize what we were signing up for. Two chronic illnesses, a federal prison sentence, and a loss of a career among the "normal" marriage hurdles. I've heard that 85 percent of marriages dissolve due to long-term incarceration. Celebrating the 15 percent with you. Our relationship makes me stronger, it makes me appreciate the small things in life, it keeps me sharp, and it makes me continually chase after our love story. The first twelve years may not be the way we would have written it; I'm intrigued to see what God will do with the next twelve and beyond.

Jameel. You've shown me grace and mercy that is second only to our Lord and Savior, Jesus Christ. Thank you for the humility it takes to tell this hard story, repeatedly. We've seen so many people's lives radically restored, because you chose to let it go and listen to God. Thank you for your Chrislike example of forgiveness.

From Jameel

I would like to thank God for allowing such an opportunity and for keeping me to do great things.

My parents, Birda and Richard McGee, for putting up with a lot of my bad decision-making—my mother especially for introducing us to Christ—and for being good parents. I am who I am because of you.

My grandmother, Rebecca McGee, for being my rock when everything else crumbled. The things you taught us we still use today.

My brothers and sisters, I love you dearly. Too many to name. Words can't describe how much you guys mean to me—a bond never broken.

My son, Jacarius McKinney-McGee, you are my light when I'm dark! You gave me reason to change my life. I want the best for you, so I need to better myself. I thank God for you, and I love you.

Latakeila McKinney, I thank you for being a mother to our son and teaching him to be a young man while I was away.

To all my aunts and uncles, friends and family, I love you all and appreciate you, and I encourage you to do something different with your life as you know it. Let God use it.

Drew, Wes, Mark, and team—love you guys! Glad to have met you all. God makes no mistakes in his plan, or who he puts in our lives.

Jobs for Life and staff, I'm so grateful to have been a part of that class, which helped me in many ways.

Overflow Church, I thank you guys for opening your doors not only to me but also to our community, for a better community moving toward greatness.